The Huge Book of Captivating Facts

by
Jake Jacobs

* * * * *

Published by Jake Jacobs

The Huge Book of Captivating Facts

1.

Hoover Dam, officially known as the Boulder Dam, is located on the border between Arizona and Nevada, USA.

2.

It was constructed between 1931 and 1936 during the Great Depression.

3.

The dam was built to control flooding, provide water storage, and generate hydroelectric power.

4.

It is named after Herbert Hoover, the 31st President of the United States.

5.

Hoover Dam is an arch-gravity dam, which means it uses both the weight of the dam and its arch-like shape to support the tremendous water pressure.

6.

It was the tallest dam in the world when it was completed, standing at 726 feet (221 meters) high.

7.

The dam impounds the Colorado River, creating Lake Mead, which is one of the largest man-made lakes in the United States.

8.

Hoover Dam is made of more than 3 million cubic yards (2.3 million cubic meters) of concrete.

9.

The dam's construction required the excavation of approximately 4.4 million cubic yards (3.4 million cubic meters) of rock and soil.

10.

Hoover Dam's power plant has 17 generators, with a total capacity of over 2,000 megawatts.

11.

It provides electricity to millions of people in Nevada, Arizona, and California.

12.

The dam's construction employed thousands of workers, who lived in a temporary settlement called "Ragtown" during the construction period.

13.

Over 100 lives were lost during the construction of Hoover Dam.

14.

The dam was a marvel of engineering at the time, utilizing advanced construction techniques and equipment.

15.

Hoover Dam was designated as a National Historic Landmark in 1985.

16.

It attracts millions of visitors each year who come to admire its impressive size and engineering feat.

17.

The dam's iconic curved shape and Art Deco style have made it a popular subject for photographs and films.

18.

The bypass bridge, known as the Mike O'Callaghan-Pat Tillman Memorial Bridge, was constructed in 2010 to alleviate traffic congestion and provide scenic views of the dam.

19.

Hoover Dam played a vital role in the development of the American Southwest, providing water and power for agriculture, industry, and urban areas.

20.

The dam's construction required the relocation of communities, including the town of St. Thomas, which was submerged under Lake Mead.

21.

It took five years to fill Lake Mead after the completion of Hoover Dam.

22.

The Hoover Dam is an important source of water for cities like Las Vegas, which relies heavily on Lake Mead for its water supply.

23.

The dam's construction was considered a significant achievement of President Franklin D. Roosevelt's New Deal program.

24.

Hoover Dam was featured in many films, including the iconic scene in the movie "Superman" where Superman saves Lois Lane from falling off the dam.

25.

The dam has a visitor center that offers tours, exhibits, and a movie about the construction and operation of the dam.

26.

It is estimated that over 1 million people have taken the guided tour of the dam since it opened to the public.

27.

The weight of the water behind Hoover Dam creates a pressure of about 45,000 pounds per square foot (2,043 kilograms per square meter) at the base of the dam.

28.

The dam's construction required the installation of approximately 582 miles (937 kilometers) of cooling pipes to dissipate the heat generated by the curing concrete.

29.

Hoover Dam's power generation contributes to the reduction of greenhouse gas emissions by providing a clean and renewable source of energy.

30.

The dam's spillways, used to release excess water during periods of heavy rainfall or snowmelt, are capable of releasing water at a rate of 450,000 cubic feet per second (12,742 cubic meters per second).

31.

Hoover Dam was one of the largest public works projects of its time, employing advanced engineering techniques and innovative construction methods.

32.

The dam's construction was a dangerous endeavor, with workers facing extreme heat, high-altitude conditions, and the risk of injury or death from accidents.

33.

The construction of Hoover Dam required the diversion of the Colorado River, creating a temporary channel for the river to flow through while the dam was being built.

34.

The dam's construction was completed two years ahead of schedule, a testament to the efficiency and dedication of the workers involved.

35.

The dam's construction cost approximately $49 million, which was funded by the federal government and repaid through the sale of hydroelectric power.

36.

Hoover Dam's generators produce enough electricity to power about 1.3 million households.

37.

The dam's construction led to the creation of a new town, Boulder City, to accommodate the workers and their families.

38.

The dam's construction required the installation of approximately 582 miles (937 kilometers) of steel pipes to carry the chilled water needed for concrete production.

39.

The dam's intake towers, which allow water to flow into the power plant, are 395 feet (120 meters) tall.

40.

The water level in Lake Mead, behind Hoover Dam, can fluctuate significantly due to droughts and water demand, affecting the dam's power generation capacity.

41.

The construction of Hoover Dam required the excavation of more than 6 million cubic yards (4.6 million cubic meters) of rock and sediment.

42.

The dam's construction created numerous jobs during the Great Depression and provided much-needed income for families in the region.

43.

Hoover Dam has become an important symbol of American engineering prowess and a testament to human ingenuity.

44.

The dam's construction required the placement of more than 200,000 cubic yards (153,000 cubic meters) of concrete in a single continuous pour for the foundation.

45.

Hoover Dam's spillways have only been used a few times in its history, most notably during the record flooding of the Colorado River in 1983.

46.

The dam's construction involved the use of over 5 million barrels of cement, enough to build a two-lane highway from San Francisco to New York City.

47.

The construction of Hoover Dam required the installation of approximately 2.4 million cubic yards (1.8 million cubic meters) of gravel and sand for the concrete mix.

48.

The dam's construction involved the placement of more than 4.4 million cubic yards (3.4 million cubic meters) of concrete, enough to build a sidewalk around the Earth's equator.

49.

Hoover Dam's construction had a significant impact on the Colorado River ecosystem, altering the natural flow of the river and affecting the habitats of various species.

50.

The construction of Hoover Dam was a remarkable feat of engineering and a testament to human determination and innovation.

51.

Hubbell Trading Post is located in Ganado, Arizona, USA, and is one of the oldest continuously operating trading posts on the Navajo Nation.

52.

It was established in 1878 by John Lorenzo Hubbell, who served as a trader and a diplomat between the Navajo people and the US government.

53.

Hubbell Trading Post played a crucial role in the cultural and economic exchange between the Navajo people and the surrounding communities.

54.

The trading post served as a hub for the exchange of goods, including wool, livestock, vegetables, and handcrafted Navajo rugs and jewelry.

55.

The original trading post building was constructed in 1878 and still stands today, preserving its historic architecture and atmosphere.

56.

Hubbell Trading Post was designated a National Historic Site in 1965, recognizing its significance in preserving the history and culture of the Navajo people.

57.

The trading post is managed by the National Park Service and operates as a living museum, showcasing the traditional trading practices and the artistry of the Navajo people.

58.

Visitors to Hubbell Trading Post can explore the historic building, browse through a vast collection of Navajo rugs and jewelry, and learn about the history and culture of the Navajo Nation.

59.

The trading post continues to operate as a place of commerce, providing a platform for Navajo artisans to sell their handcrafted goods.

60.

Hubbell Trading Post offers guided tours, educational programs, and demonstrations of traditional Navajo weaving and silversmithing techniques.

61.

The trading post also hosts special events, including cultural celebrations, art shows, and lectures, promoting the preservation and understanding of Navajo culture.

62.

The trading post is surrounded by beautiful landscapes, including red rock formations and picturesque desert scenery, offering visitors a unique and immersive experience.

63.

Hubbell Trading Post is known for its exceptional collection of Navajo rugs, which showcase intricate designs and vibrant colors, reflecting the artistry and craftsmanship of the Navajo weavers.

64.

The trading post played a significant role in the revival of traditional Navajo rug weaving, providing a market for the weavers' creations and encouraging the preservation of this cultural tradition.

65.

Hubbell Trading Post has been featured in several films and documentaries, further highlighting its historical and cultural importance.

66.

The trading post serves as a cultural bridge, fostering understanding and appreciation between the Navajo people and visitors from around the world.

67.

The surrounding area offers opportunities for outdoor activities, including hiking, birdwatching, and exploring the scenic landscapes of the Navajo Nation.

68.

Hubbell Trading Post stands as a testament to the enduring legacy of John Lorenzo Hubbell and his commitment to promoting cultural exchange and economic development in the region.

69.

The trading post's interior is filled with historical artifacts, photographs, and displays that provide insights into the rich history and traditions of the Navajo people.

70.

Hubbell Trading Post is a popular destination for collectors and enthusiasts of Native American art and artifacts, offering a wide range of authentic and high-quality pieces.

71.

The trading post's location in Ganado provides visitors with the opportunity to explore the unique culture and traditions of the Navajo people, including attending local ceremonies and events.

72.

Hubbell Trading Post has been recognized as a National Historic Landmark, highlighting its significance in American history and its contribution to preserving Native American heritage.

73.

The trading post has a small museum that showcases a variety of items, including pottery, baskets, and traditional Navajo clothing, providing a comprehensive look into Navajo culture.

74.

Hubbell Trading Post offers educational programs for schools and groups, providing an immersive learning experience about Navajo history, weaving techniques, and traditional practices.

75.

The trading post's location near the Four Corners region allows visitors to explore nearby attractions such as Canyon de Chelly National Monument and Monument Valley.

76.

Hubbell Trading Post has a visitor center where visitors can obtain information, purchase souvenirs, and learn about upcoming events and programs.

77.

The trading post has been passed down through generations of the Hubbell family, with the current generation actively involved in the preservation and promotion of Navajo culture.

78.

Hubbell Trading Post showcases the intricate craftsmanship of Navajo silversmiths, with a wide selection of silver jewelry featuring traditional designs and motifs.

79.

The trading post offers demonstrations of traditional Navajo rug weaving, allowing visitors to witness the skill and precision required to create these exquisite works of art.

80.

Hubbell Trading Post is a place of cultural exchange, where visitors can engage in meaningful conversations with Navajo artisans and gain insights into their traditions and way of life.

81.

The trading post hosts workshops and classes on Navajo weaving and silversmithing, providing opportunities for visitors to learn and participate in these traditional arts.

82.

Hubbell Trading Post has a tranquil and serene atmosphere, making it an ideal place for reflection, appreciation of Native American culture, and connection with nature.

83.

The trading post offers a variety of guided tours, including tours focused on the history of the trading post, the art of Navajo rug weaving, and the natural beauty of the surrounding landscape.

84.

Hubbell Trading Post features a gift shop where visitors can purchase authentic Navajo rugs, jewelry, pottery, and other handcrafted items, supporting local artisans and the Navajo economy.

85.

The trading post has a picnic area where visitors can relax and enjoy their meals while surrounded by the peacefulness of the Navajo reservation.

86.

Hubbell Trading Post celebrates the Navajo way of life through cultural demonstrations, storytelling, and traditional music and dance performances.

87.

The trading post offers interpretive programs that delve into the history and significance of Hubbell Trading Post, providing a deeper understanding of its role in Navajo and American history.

88.

Hubbell Trading Post has been featured in numerous publications and media outlets, bringing attention to its cultural importance and attracting visitors from around the world.

89.

The trading post's architecture reflects a blend of Navajo and Spanish influences, showcasing the unique cultural heritage of the region.

90.

Hubbell Trading Post has been recognized as an important site for the preservation of traditional Navajo weaving techniques, contributing to the UNESCO's Intangible Cultural Heritage list.

91.

The trading post offers opportunities for visitors to participate in traditional Navajo activities, such as rug weaving workshops and Navajo cooking classes.

92.

Hubbell Trading Post holds special events throughout the year, including art exhibits, storytelling nights, and cultural festivals, providing a vibrant and dynamic experience for visitors.

93.

The trading post's location within the Navajo Nation allows visitors to learn about the tribe's governance, traditions, and ongoing efforts to preserve their language and culture.

94.

Hubbell Trading Post has an extensive library and archive that houses historical documents, photographs, and recordings related to the trading post and the Navajo people.

95.

The trading post's courtyard serves as a gathering place for visitors and locals, fostering a sense of community and cultural exchange.

96.

Hubbell Trading Post offers guided hikes and nature walks in the surrounding area, allowing visitors to explore the natural beauty of the region while learning about its ecological significance.

97.

The trading post collaborates with local schools and educational institutions to provide educational programs that promote cultural understanding and appreciation.

98.

Hubbell Trading Post is a popular destination for photographers, offering stunning views of the surrounding landscape and opportunities to capture the rich cultural heritage of the Navajo people.

99.

The trading post's gardens feature traditional Navajo plants and herbs, providing a glimpse into the Navajo people's use of natural resources for food, medicine, and ceremonies.

100.

Hubbell Trading Post stands as a testament to the resilience and ingenuity of the Navajo people, serving as a bridge between their past and future generations, and preserving their cultural identity.

101.

Thomas Nelson Jr. was born on December 26, 1738, in Yorktown, Virginia.

102.

Nelson came from a prominent Virginia family, with his father serving as a colonial governor.

103.

He received his education at the College of William and Mary and later studied law in England.

104.

Nelson served as a delegate to the Continental Congress from 1775 to 1777 and again from 1779 to 1781.

105.

He was an active participant in the American Revolutionary War and served as a brigadier general in the Virginia militia.

106.

Nelson played a crucial role in the Battle of Yorktown, where he commanded the Virginia militia and helped secure victory for the American forces.

107.

As a signer of the Declaration of Independence, Nelson pledged his life, fortune, and sacred honor to the cause of American independence.

108.

Nelson was a staunch supporter of states' rights and was involved in the debate over the ratification of the United States Constitution.

109.

He served as governor of Virginia from 1781 to 1782, during a critical period of the state's history.

110.

Nelson was known for his strong advocacy for religious freedom and played a key role in the passage of the Virginia Statute for Religious Freedom.

111.

Despite his contributions to the American Revolution, Nelson faced financial hardships and personal sacrifices.

112.

During the war, Nelson lent a large sum of money to the American cause, which he never fully recovered.

113.

His home in Yorktown, known as the Nelson House, served as the headquarters for both British and American commanders during the Siege of Yorktown.

114.

Nelson was a skilled and successful merchant, engaging in various business ventures, including trade and shipping.

115.

He was a member of the Virginia House of Burgesses, representing York County, and later served in the Virginia Senate.

116.

Nelson was a strong advocate for the abolition of slavery and took steps to emancipate his own enslaved individuals.

117.

Nelson was an avid supporter of education and served as a trustee for several educational institutions.

118.

He was a founding member of the American Philosophical Society, a learned society dedicated to the promotion of scientific knowledge.

119.

Nelson had a keen interest in horticulture and maintained a beautiful garden at his Yorktown estate.

120.

Nelson had a close friendship with fellow Virginian and founding father Thomas Jefferson, with whom he shared political and philosophical views.

121.

Nelson's health deteriorated in his later years, and he suffered from various ailments, including gout.

122.

He died on January 4, 1789, at the age of 50 and was buried at the Grace Churchyard in Yorktown.

123.

Nelson's legacy lives on in the Thomas Nelson Community College in Hampton, Virginia, which was named in his honor.

124.

The Nelson County in Virginia was also named after him as a tribute to his contributions to the state and the nation.

125.

Nelson's descendants continued to play significant roles in American history, with several serving as prominent politicians and military officers.

126.

Nelson's son, Hugh Nelson, served as a congressman and diplomat, representing Virginia in the U.S. House of Representatives.

127.

Another son, William Nelson, served as a lieutenant colonel in the Continental Army and later as governor of Virginia.

128.

Nelson's grandson, Thomas Nelson Jr., became the governor of Virginia and served as a U.S. senator.

129.

Nelson's great-grandson, Thomas Nelson Page, was a well-known author and diplomat.

130.

Nelson's contributions to the American Revolution were honored by the U.S. Postal Service with the issuance of a commemorative stamp in 1975.

131.

Nelson's personal papers and correspondence provide valuable insights into the political and social climate of colonial and Revolutionary-era Virginia.

132.

Nelson's commitment to the ideals of liberty and independence remains an inspiration to future generations of Americans.

133.

The Thomas Nelson House in Williamsburg, Virginia, serves as a museum dedicated to preserving the history and legacy of the Nelson family.

134.

Nelson's leadership and dedication during the Revolutionary War helped shape the course of American history.

135.

His role in the Battle of Yorktown is considered instrumental in securing American independence.

136.

Nelson's public service and commitment to the welfare of Virginia earned him the respect and admiration of his contemporaries.

137.

Nelson's wealth and status did not hinder his willingness to put his own resources at risk for the cause of American liberty.

138.

Nelson's political career was marked by his unwavering support for the principles of self-governance and individual rights.

139.

He was known for his eloquence and persuasive speaking abilities, which he used to rally support for the American cause.

140.

Nelson's dedication to religious freedom helped shape the values enshrined in the First Amendment to the United States Constitution.

141.

His contributions to the development of Virginia's legal and political systems laid the groundwork for future generations.

142.

Nelson's commitment to public service extended beyond his role as a statesman, as he actively participated in community affairs and charitable endeavors.

143.

Nelson's leadership and integrity made him a trusted and respected figure among his peers.

144.

His actions during the American Revolution demonstrated his unwavering commitment to the principles of liberty and self-determination.

145.

Nelson's service as governor of Virginia during a challenging period showcased his ability to navigate complex political situations.

146.

He played a crucial role in fostering unity among the states and strengthening the bonds of the young nation.

147.

Nelson's support for agriculture and trade contributed to the economic growth and prosperity of Virginia.

148.

He advocated for the establishment of public schools and the promotion of education as a means of fostering an informed and engaged citizenry.

149.

Nelson's contributions to the American Revolution earned him a place among the esteemed founding fathers of the United States.

150.

His life and legacy serve as a reminder of the sacrifices made by those who fought for American independence and the principles upon which the nation was founded.

151.

William Paca was born on October 31, 1740, in Abingdon, Maryland.

152.

He was the son of wealthy parents and received an excellent education, attending the College of Philadelphia (now the University of Pennsylvania).

153.

Paca studied law and was admitted to the bar in 1761, establishing a successful legal practice in Annapolis, Maryland.

154.

He became actively involved in the patriot cause and was a member of the Annapolis Convention in 1774, which called for a boycott of British goods.

155.

Paca was a strong supporter of American independence and served as a delegate to the Continental Congress from 1774 to 1779.

156.

He signed the Declaration of Independence in 1776, pledging his life, fortune, and sacred honor to the cause of American liberty.

157.

Paca played a key role in Maryland politics, serving as a delegate to the Maryland State Constitutional Convention in 1776 and helping to draft the state's first constitution.

158.

He served as the governor of Maryland from 1782 to 1785, during which he worked to stabilize the state's finances and promote economic growth.

159.

As governor, Paca advocated for religious freedom and supported the disestablishment of the Anglican Church in Maryland.

160.

Paca was a proponent of education and helped establish St. John's College in Annapolis, which is still in operation today.

161.

He was also involved in the formation of the Maryland Society for Promoting the Abolition of Slavery and the Relief of Free Negroes and Others Unlawfully Held in Bondage.

162.

Paca was a strong advocate for agricultural development and promoted scientific farming methods in Maryland.

163.

He was an early supporter of the Society of the Cincinnati, a fraternal organization for Revolutionary War officers.

164.

After leaving office as governor, Paca continued to serve his community as a judge, holding positions in both the state and federal courts.

165.

He was appointed as a federal district judge by President George Washington in 1789 and served in that role until his death.

166.

Paca was a close friend and ally of several prominent figures of the time, including Thomas Jefferson and John Adams.

167.

He maintained an extensive correspondence with fellow patriots and kept detailed records of his experiences and observations.

168.

Paca was a skilled horticulturist and took great pride in his gardens at his Annapolis estate, known as Wye Hall.

169.

He was interested in botany and collected a wide variety of plants, many of which were rare or exotic for the time.

170.

Paca's gardens were renowned for their beauty and were often visited by distinguished guests, including Marquis de Lafayette.

171.

He was a founding member of the American Philosophical Society, a learned society that promotes the advancement of knowledge.

172.

Paca was a strong advocate for the ratification of the United States Constitution and actively campaigned for its adoption in Maryland.

173.

He served as a delegate to the Maryland Ratifying Convention in 1788, where he argued in favor of the Constitution's merits.

174.

Paca's dedication to public service extended beyond politics, as he was involved in various charitable and civic organizations.

175.

He helped establish the Maryland Historical Society, which aimed to preserve the state's rich history and promote historical research.

176.

Paca's health declined in his later years, and he suffered from gout and other chronic ailments.

177.

He died on October 23, 1799, at the age of 58 and was buried at Wye Hall.

178.

Paca's legacy is commemorated in various ways, including the naming of Paca Street in Annapolis and the William Paca Garden in Philadelphia.

179.

His former home, Wye Hall, still stands today and is open to the public as a museum and historic site.

180.

Paca's contributions to the American Revolution and the founding of the nation are recognized and celebrated by historians and scholars.

181.

His signature on the Declaration of Independence symbolizes his commitment to the principles of liberty and self-determination.

182.

Paca's writings and speeches provide valuable insights into the political and social climate of the Revolutionary era.

183.

He was known for his eloquence and persuasive speaking abilities, which helped shape public opinion in support of independence.

184.

Paca's legal expertise and commitment to justice made him a respected figure in the legal community.

185.

He was known for his fair and impartial rulings as a judge, earning the trust and admiration of his colleagues and constituents.

186.

Paca's contributions to the development of Maryland's legal system and governance laid the foundation for future generations.

187.

His commitment to religious freedom and the separation of church and state helped shape the values enshrined in the First Amendment.

188.

Paca's dedication to public service and the common good set a precedent for future leaders in Maryland and beyond.

189.

He was a staunch defender of individual rights and limited government, advocating for a balance of power between the state and federal governments.

190.

Paca's commitment to agriculture and scientific farming methods contributed to the economic growth and prosperity of Maryland.

191.

He believed in the importance of education and worked to expand educational opportunities for all Marylanders.

192.

Paca's contributions to the abolitionist movement in Maryland helped lay the groundwork for the eventual abolition of slavery in the state.

193.

He was a man of integrity and moral character, known for his honesty, loyalty, and dedication to the principles of liberty and justice.

194.

Paca's leadership during a pivotal time in American history helped shape the course of the nation and secure its independence.

195.

His commitment to public service and the greater good of society continues to inspire future generations of leaders.

196.

Paca's life and legacy are commemorated in various historical markers, monuments, and museums throughout Maryland.

197.

He is remembered as a patriot and statesman who played a vital role in the founding of the United States.

198.

Paca's contributions to the fields of law, politics, and agriculture exemplify his versatility and broad range of interests.

199.

He was known for his meticulous attention to detail and careful consideration of the consequences of his actions.

200.

Paca's commitment to the principles of liberty, justice, and equality serve as a reminder of the ideals upon which the nation was founded.

201.

Bengal tigers (Panthera tigris tigris) are the most numerous tiger subspecies and are found primarily in India and Bangladesh.

202.

They are known for their striking orange coat with black stripes, which provides excellent camouflage in their forested habitats.

203.

Bengal tigers are the national animal of both India and Bangladesh.

204.

Males are larger than females, with an average length of 8-10 feet (2.5-3 meters) and a weight of 400-550 pounds (180-250 kilograms).

205.

They are powerful hunters and can take down large prey, including deer, wild boar, and buffalo.

206.

Bengal tigers have excellent eyesight and hearing, which help them locate prey in their dense forest environment.

207.

They are solitary animals, with males occupying larger home ranges that overlap with several female territories.

208.

Bengal tigers are highly territorial and mark their territory with scent markings and vocalizations.

209.

They are excellent swimmers and often take to the water to cool off or hunt for prey.

210.

Bengal tigers have strong jaws and can deliver a powerful bite, capable of crushing bones.

211.

They have retractable claws that they use for gripping prey and climbing trees.

212.

Bengal tigers are known for their distinct roar, which can be heard over long distances.

213.

They are apex predators and play a crucial role in maintaining the ecological balance of their habitat.

214.

Female Bengal tigers give birth to a litter of 2-4 cubs after a gestation period of around 100 days.

215.

The cubs are born blind and rely on their mother for nourishment and protection.

216.

Bengal tigers are excellent mothers and will fiercely defend their cubs from any potential threats.

217.

Cubs start hunting with their mother at around 18 months and become fully independent by the age of 2-2.5 years.

218.

Bengal tigers have a lifespan of 10-15 years in the wild, but can live longer in captivity.

219.

They are classified as endangered by the International Union for Conservation of Nature (IUCN) due to habitat loss and poaching.

220.

Conservation efforts, such as the establishment of protected areas and anti-poaching initiatives, are crucial for their survival.

221.

The Sundarbans, a mangrove forest in Bangladesh and India, is home to the largest population of Bengal tigers.

222.

Bengal tigers are excellent climbers and often rest or scan their surroundings from tree branches.

223.

They have a keen sense of smell, which helps them locate prey and potential mates.

224.

Bengal tigers are crepuscular animals, meaning they are most active during dawn and dusk.

225.

They have been known to occasionally prey on humans, usually due to habitat encroachment and scarcity of natural prey.

226.

In Hindu mythology, the Bengal tiger is associated with the goddess Durga and is considered a symbol of power and strength.

227.

Bengal tigers have a distinct coat pattern, with each individual having unique stripe patterns, similar to human fingerprints.

228.

They are capable of running at speeds of up to 40 miles per hour (65 kilometers per hour) for short distances.

229.

Bengal tigers have a specialized hunting technique known as "stalk and ambush," where they patiently stalk their prey before launching a surprise attack.

230.

Their coat coloration provides effective camouflage in the tall grasses and dense forests where they hunt.

231.

Bengal tigers have been depicted in various forms of art and literature, symbolizing beauty, grace, and strength.

232.

They are known for their ability to leap long distances, allowing them to pounce on unsuspecting prey.

233.

Bengal tigers have well-developed muscles in their forelimbs, which enable them to bring down large prey.

234.

They are capable of consuming large amounts of food in a single sitting, sometimes consuming up to 40 kilograms (88 pounds) of meat at once.

235.

Bengal tigers have an average hunting success rate of around 10-20%, as they rely on stealth and surprise to catch their prey.

236.

They have a series of whiskers on their face called "vibrissae," which are highly sensitive and help them navigate in low-light conditions.

237.

Bengal tigers have a specialized vocalization called a "chuff," which is used for communication between individuals.

238.

They have a complex social structure, with individuals establishing dominance hierarchies within their territories.

239.

Bengal tigers have a unique cooling mechanism in their tongues, with blood vessels that help regulate their body temperature in hot climates.

240.

They are highly adaptable and can inhabit a variety of habitats, including grasslands, mangroves, and subtropical forests.

241.

Bengal tigers are excellent swimmers and can cross large rivers and swim between islands.

242.

They have large paws with retractable claws, which help them navigate different types of terrain and make quick turns while chasing prey.

243.

Bengal tigers play an important role in eco-tourism, attracting visitors from around the world to see these majestic animals in their natural habitat.

244.

They are known for their stealthy and silent movements, allowing them to approach prey undetected.

245.

Bengal tigers have a keen sense of hearing, which helps them locate prey even in dense vegetation.

246.

They have a specialized dental structure, with sharp canines and molars designed for tearing flesh and crushing bones.

247.

Bengal tigers have been the subject of numerous conservation and research efforts aimed at protecting their population and habitat.

248.

They are considered a flagship species for conservation, as their survival depends on the preservation of their natural habitat and the protection of other wildlife species in the ecosystem.

249.

Bengal tigers are excellent climbers and are capable of scaling trees to escape floodwaters or to get a better vantage point.

250.

They have a low population density compared to other tiger subspecies, with an estimated 2,500-3,000 individuals remaining in the wild.

251.

Betta fish, scientifically known as Betta splendens, are popular freshwater aquarium fish native to Southeast Asia.

252.

They are known for their vibrant colors and elaborate fins, making them a visually striking fish species.

253.

Betta fish have been selectively bred over the years, resulting in a wide variety of color patterns and fin shapes.

254.

Male bettas are known for their territorial and aggressive behavior, which is why they are often kept alone in aquariums.

255.

Female bettas can also display aggression towards each other but are generally less aggressive than males.

256.

Betta fish have a labyrinth organ, which allows them to breathe air from the water's surface, in addition to using their gills.

257.

This unique adaptation enables them to survive in oxygen-deprived environments such as stagnant ponds and rice paddies.

258.

Betta fish come in various colors, including red, blue, green, yellow, and purple, among others.

259.

The fins of a betta fish can be long and flowing, or short and rounded, depending on the breed.

260.

In the wild, bettas inhabit shallow rice paddies, slow-moving streams, and stagnant waters with dense vegetation.

261.

They are known for their nest-building behavior, with males constructing bubble nests at the water's surface to protect and incubate their eggs.

262.

Betta fish are carnivorous and primarily feed on insects, larvae, and small crustaceans in their natural habitat.

263.

In captivity, bettas are usually fed a diet of high-quality pellet or flake food specially formulated for their nutritional needs.

264.

They have an upturned mouth that allows them to eat food from the water's surface more easily.

265.

Betta fish have excellent vision and can see in color, which helps them navigate their environment and locate prey.

266.

They are known for their unique courtship behavior, where the male performs a display to attract the female's attention.

267.

During courtship, the male betta flares his fins and displays vibrant colors to impress the female.

268.

Once the female accepts the male's courtship, they engage in a brief spawning ritual, where the female releases eggs and the male fertilizes them.

269.

Betta fish eggs are adhesive and will stick to the bubble nest, which the male then guards and tends to until the fry hatch.

270.

The male betta exhibits parental care by protecting the nest, removing any fallen eggs, and ensuring the fry have a suitable environment to grow.

271.

Betta fish have a lifespan of around 2-4 years on average, although some can live longer with proper care.

272.

They are resilient fish and can tolerate a range of water conditions, but it's important to provide them with clean water and proper filtration.

273.

Betta fish are known for their ability to "flare," where they expand their fins and gill covers to display aggression or establish dominance.

274.

They have a labyrinth organ that allows them to survive in water with low oxygen levels, but they still require regular water changes to maintain good health.

275.

Betta fish are jumpers and can leap out of open aquariums, so it's essential to provide a secure lid or cover for their tank.

276.

They are highly interactive fish and can recognize their owners, often responding to their presence by swimming towards them.

277.

Betta fish have a unique personality, with some individuals being more outgoing and curious than others.

278.

They are known for their ability to recognize patterns and even learn simple tricks with positive reinforcement training.

279.

Betta fish have a sensitive lateral line system, which helps them detect water movement and changes in their environment.

280.

They are susceptible to various diseases, including fin rot, ich, and velvet, so it's important to maintain good water quality and provide proper care to prevent illness.

281.

Betta fish are sensitive to temperature fluctuations and thrive in water temperatures between 76-82°F (24-28°C).

282.

They prefer aquariums with hiding places, such as caves or plants, where they can retreat and feel secure.

283.

Betta fish are known to display territorial behavior, especially towards other bettas or fish with similar appearances.

284.

They have a labyrinth organ located behind their gills, which allows them to breathe atmospheric air.

285.

The labyrinth organ is lined with specialized tissue that facilitates oxygen exchange, allowing bettas to survive in oxygen-deprived waters.

286.

Betta fish have been bred for specific traits, resulting in various tail types such as veil tail, crowntail, halfmoon, delta, and plakat.

287.

They are popular pets for beginners and experienced fish keepers due to their striking appearance and relative ease of care.

288.

Betta fish are skilled jumpers and can leap several inches out of the water, so it's important to provide a well-fitted lid on their tank.

289.

They are highly territorial and should not be housed with other aggressive or fin-nipping fish species.

290.

Betta fish are capable of recognizing their reflection in a mirror and may display aggressive behavior towards their own reflection.

291.

They have a unique sleeping behavior where they rest on the surface or near the water's surface, often appearing motionless.

292.

Betta fish have a labyrinth organ that enables them to survive in poorly oxygenated water, such as puddles or rice fields during the dry season.

293.

They are known for their ability to change color temporarily, especially in response to stress, excitement, or changes in their environment.

294.

The vibrant colors of betta fish are derived from pigments called chromatophores present in their skin cells.

295.

Betta fish exhibit a wide range of color variations, including solid colors, marbled patterns, and iridescent scales.

296.

They have excellent hearing capabilities and can detect vibrations in the water, allowing them to locate potential prey or threats.

297.

Betta fish have a relatively small stomach compared to their body size, so it's important to feed them small, frequent meals rather than a large amount at once.

298.

They are intelligent fish and can learn to recognize feeding times and respond to cues from their owners.

299.

Betta fish have a unique organ called the "macrophage," which helps them fight off infections and heal wounds.

300.

They are popular subjects for artists and photographers due to their vibrant colors, flowing fins, and graceful swimming movements.

301.

The Jerome Historic District is located in Jerome, Arizona, and is a National Historic Landmark.

302.

The town of Jerome was once a bustling copper mining town and is now known as the "Wickedest Town in the West."

303.

The district encompasses the entire town of Jerome, covering an area of approximately 300 acres.

304.

Jerome is situated on the side of Cleopatra Hill and offers stunning views of the surrounding Verde Valley.

305.

The historic district is known for its steep and winding streets, as well as its unique architecture and colorful buildings.

306.

Many of the buildings in Jerome were constructed during the late 19th century and early 20th century, showcasing a mix of architectural styles, including Victorian, Gothic Revival, and Spanish Colonial Revival.

307.

The district is home to several historic landmarks, including the Jerome State Historic Park, Douglas Mansion, and the Jerome Grand Hotel.

308.

Jerome was once one of the largest copper mining towns in the United States, with a population of over 15,000 during its peak.

309.

The town experienced several booms and busts throughout its history, with the mining industry being the primary source of economic activity.

310.

In the early 20th century, Jerome faced significant challenges, including fires, landslides, and labor strikes.

311.

The town's population declined dramatically in the mid-20th century, and by the 1950s, it was almost a ghost town.

312.

In the 1960s, artists and hippies began to move into the abandoned buildings of Jerome, leading to a revitalization of the town.

313.

Today, Jerome is a thriving tourist destination known for its art galleries, shops, restaurants, and vibrant arts community.

314.

The district is home to several museums and art galleries that showcase the town's rich history and artistic heritage.

315.

Jerome is famous for its paranormal activity and is considered one of the most haunted towns in America.

316.

Visitors can take ghost tours to learn about the town's eerie past and stories of supernatural encounters.

317.

The district is a popular destination for photography enthusiasts due to its unique architecture, stunning landscapes, and dramatic sunsets.

318.

The town has been featured in several movies and television shows, including "Four Faces West" and "Ghost Adventures."

319.

Jerome holds an annual "Ghost Walk" event, where visitors can explore the town's haunted history and participate in ghostly activities.

320.

The district offers numerous hiking trails, including the popular "Sliding Jail Trail," which takes visitors past the remnants of the town's old jail that slid down the hillside.

321.

The district is surrounded by beautiful natural scenery, including the Prescott National Forest and the Verde River.

322.

Jerome was designated as a National Historic Landmark in 1976 for its significant historical and architectural importance.

323.

The Jerome Historic District is home to a vibrant community of artists, writers, and musicians who draw inspiration from the town's unique atmosphere.

324.

The town's economy has diversified beyond mining, with tourism playing a significant role in sustaining the local businesses.

325.

The Jerome Historic District has been recognized for its commitment to historic preservation and sustainable development.

326.

The district hosts several annual events, including the Jerome Art Walk, the Jerome Indie Film & Music Festival, and the Jerome Historic Home and Building Tour.

327.

The town's narrow streets and steep inclines add to its charm and create a sense of adventure for visitors exploring the district.

328.

Jerome is known for its vibrant nightlife, with numerous bars, restaurants, and live music venues catering to locals and tourists.

329.

The district offers a variety of accommodations, including charming bed and breakfasts, historic hotels, and vacation rentals.

330.

Jerome is a popular destination for motorcycle enthusiasts who enjoy riding through the winding mountain roads surrounding the town.

331.

The town's unique geography and architectural features have made it a popular filming location for commercials and music videos.

332.

Jerome has its own local newspaper, "The Jerome News," which covers community events, news, and stories of local interest.

333.

The district is home to several art studios and workshops where visitors can observe artists at work and purchase unique creations.

334.

Jerome's vibrant community hosts regular events, including live music performances, theater productions, and art exhibitions.

335.

The district's rich mining history can be explored through the various exhibits and displays at the Jerome State Historic Park.

336.

Jerome has a strong sense of community, with residents actively involved in preserving the town's heritage and promoting sustainable practices.

337.

The district offers stunning panoramic views of the surrounding mountains and valleys, making it a favorite spot for landscape photographers.

338.

The town has its own fire department, police force, and post office, serving the needs of both residents and visitors.

339.

Jerome has several parks and outdoor recreational areas where visitors can enjoy picnicking, hiking, and wildlife spotting.

340.

The district is home to unique shops and boutiques offering a range of merchandise, including local crafts, jewelry, and vintage items.

341.

Jerome has a rich cultural history, with a diverse population that has contributed to the town's unique character and traditions.

342.

The district's streets are lined with colorful flower displays, adding to the town's charm and beauty.

343.

Jerome is located within easy driving distance of other popular
Arizona destinations, including Sedona, Flagstaff, and the Grand
Canyon.

344.

The town's historic buildings have been meticulously preserved, with
many of them housing thriving businesses and residences.

345.

Jerome has a strong sense of environmental stewardship, with
initiatives in place to protect the surrounding natural resources.

346.

The district offers guided tours that provide in-depth information
about the town's history, architecture, and notable residents.

347.

Jerome has its own community center, where residents and visitors
can participate in various recreational and educational activities.

348.

The town's residents are proud of their unique heritage and actively
participate in community events and celebrations.

349.

Jerome has been recognized as one of the best small art towns in
America, attracting artists from around the country.

350.

The Jerome Historic District provides a fascinating glimpse into
Arizona's past and offers a memorable experience for visitors
seeking history, art, and natural beauty.

351.

Kinishba Ruins is an archaeological site located in eastern Arizona, near the town of Whiteriver.

352.

The ruins are the remains of a large pueblo village that was occupied by the ancestral Puebloan people, also known as the Mogollon culture.

353.

The site is situated on a hilltop overlooking the White River valley, offering scenic views of the surrounding landscape.

354.

Kinishba Ruins is believed to have been inhabited between the 11th and 14th centuries, with evidence of both permanent and seasonal occupation.

355.

The pueblo complex at Kinishba once consisted of over 600 rooms and multiple kivas (ceremonial underground structures).

356.

The architecture of the ruins is characterized by its unique T-shaped doorways, which are a distinctive feature of the Mogollon culture.

357.

Excavations at Kinishba have revealed artifacts such as pottery, stone tools, jewelry, and grinding stones, providing insight into the daily lives and cultural practices of the ancestral Puebloans.

358.

The site was first documented by archaeologist Byron Cummings in the early 20th century, and subsequent excavations have shed light on its significance.

359.

Kinishba Ruins is listed on the National Register of Historic Places and is recognized as a National Historic Landmark.

360.

The site is managed by the White Mountain Apache Tribe and is open to the public for tours and exploration.

361.

Visitors to Kinishba Ruins can take guided tours led by knowledgeable guides who provide insights into the site's history and cultural significance.

362.

The ruins offer an opportunity to see the well-preserved remnants of an ancient pueblo village and imagine what life was like for the ancestral Puebloan people.

363.

Kinishba Ruins is a significant archaeological site in the Southwest, contributing to our understanding of pre-Columbian Native American cultures.

364.

The surrounding landscape of Kinishba Ruins is characterized by desert vegetation, rolling hills, and scenic vistas.

365.

The site has been studied by archaeologists and anthropologists, who continue to research and interpret its history and cultural significance.

366.

Kinishba Ruins is a place of spiritual and cultural importance for the White Mountain Apache Tribe, who have ancestral connections to the site.

367.

The ruins have been the subject of archaeological investigations, including mapping, excavations, and analysis of the artifacts discovered.

368.

The pueblo architecture at Kinishba demonstrates advanced engineering techniques, including masonry construction and well-designed room layouts.

369.

Kinishba Ruins provides a glimpse into the social organization and community life of the ancestral Puebloans, who lived in multi-story structures and practiced agriculture.

370.

The site's location on a hilltop likely served both defensive and ceremonial purposes for the ancestral Puebloans.

371.

The construction materials used in the ruins include local stone, adobe, and wooden beams.

372.

Kinishba Ruins is believed to have been a regional center for trade and cultural exchange among the ancient Puebloan communities.

373.

The site's preservation has been a collaborative effort between the White Mountain Apache Tribe, archaeologists, and government agencies.

374.

Kinishba Ruins is a popular destination for photographers, offering unique opportunities to capture the beauty and history of the site.

375.

The site's visitor center provides interpretive exhibits, educational programs, and information about the ancestral Puebloan culture.

376.

Kinishba Ruins is an important place for cultural and educational programs, including workshops, lectures, and demonstrations.

377.

The ruins are surrounded by nature trails, allowing visitors to explore the archaeological site and enjoy the natural beauty of the area.

378.

Kinishba Ruins has been featured in documentaries and publications that highlight the rich history and archaeological significance of the site.

379.

The site's location in the White Mountains of Arizona provides a cooler and more temperate climate compared to the surrounding desert regions.

380.

Kinishba Ruins has been a site of ongoing research, with archaeologists and anthropologists studying its architecture, pottery styles, and cultural practices.

381.

The ruins offer an opportunity to learn about the ancestral Puebloan people's agricultural techniques, including the cultivation of corn, beans, and squash.

382.

Kinishba Ruins has served as an outdoor classroom for students and researchers interested in archaeology and Native American history.

383.

The ruins' proximity to other cultural and natural attractions in Arizona, such as the Petrified Forest National Park and the Apache-Sitgreaves National Forest, makes it a valuable stop for tourists.

384.

Kinishba Ruins provides a peaceful and serene setting, allowing visitors to connect with the ancient past and appreciate the beauty of the surrounding landscape.

385.

The site's location within the Fort Apache Indian Reservation adds to its cultural significance, highlighting the enduring presence of Native American communities in the region.

386.

Kinishba Ruins showcases the ingenuity and architectural skills of the ancestral Puebloan people, who built intricate structures without the use of modern tools and equipment.

387.

The ruins have inspired artists, writers, and photographers who seek to capture the mystique and historical significance of the site.

388.

Kinishba Ruins has been featured in archaeological publications and research papers, contributing to the broader understanding of the Mogollon culture.

389.

The site's preservation and interpretation efforts aim to foster appreciation and respect for Native American heritage and promote cultural exchange.

390.

Kinishba Ruins serves as a reminder of the enduring legacy of the ancestral Puebloan people and their contributions to the cultural tapestry of the Southwest.

391.

The ruins provide a glimpse into the religious and ceremonial practices of the ancestral Puebloans, who conducted rituals and ceremonies in the kivas.

392.

Kinishba Ruins is an example of the sustainability and adaptability of ancient civilizations, as the ancestral Puebloans thrived in the challenging desert environment.

393.

The site's significance extends beyond its archaeological value, as it serves as a symbol of Native American resilience and cultural continuity.

394.

Kinishba Ruins has been visited by scholars, researchers, and Native American leaders, who recognize its importance in preserving and sharing Indigenous history.

395.

The ruins have been the subject of oral histories and cultural traditions passed down through generations, connecting contemporary Native American communities to their ancestral roots.

396.

The site's accessibility and visitor facilities make it a family-friendly destination, where children can learn about ancient cultures and connect with the natural world.

397.

Kinishba Ruins has been a site for collaborative research and educational partnerships between archaeologists, anthropologists, and Native American communities.

398.

The ruins' remote location and peaceful ambiance make it an ideal place for meditation, reflection, and spiritual connection with the past.

399.

Kinishba Ruins has been a subject of archaeological debates and theories, stimulating discussions on topics such as population dynamics and cultural change.

400.

The site's cultural significance is recognized by the State of Arizona, which has designated Kinishba Ruins as a State Historic Site, ensuring its preservation and protection for future generations.

401.

Robert Treat Paine was born on March 11, 1731, in Boston, Massachusetts.

402.

Paine was an American lawyer, jurist, and politician who played a significant role in the American Revolution and the early years of the United States.

403.

He graduated from Harvard College in 1749 and later studied law under the renowned lawyer and future President John Adams.

404.

Paine established a successful law practice in Taunton, Massachusetts, and gained a reputation as an eloquent and persuasive speaker.

405.

In 1770, Paine served as a prosecutor in the trial of the British soldiers involved in the Boston Massacre, advocating for justice and fairness.

406.

Paine became a vocal supporter of American independence and was elected to the Massachusetts Provincial Congress in 1774.

407.

He was one of the signatories of the Declaration of Independence, affixing his signature to the historic document in 1776.

408.

Paine served as a delegate to the Continental Congress from 1774 to 1778 and again from 1780 to 1782.

409.

As a member of Congress, Paine was involved in important committees, including the committee responsible for drafting the Articles of Confederation.

410.

Paine played a crucial role in shaping the legal and political structures of the newly independent United States.

411.

In 1780, Paine was appointed Attorney General of Massachusetts, a position he held until 1790.

412.

Paine was an advocate for judicial reform and worked to improve the legal system in Massachusetts.

413.

He served as a judge of the Massachusetts Supreme Judicial Court from 1790 until his retirement in 1804.

414.

Paine was known for his strict adherence to the rule of law and his commitment to justice.

415.

In 1791, Paine argued the landmark case of Commonwealth v. Jennison before the Massachusetts Supreme Judicial Court, which established the principle of judicial review in the state.

416.

Paine was also involved in promoting education and served as a trustee of Harvard College.

417.

He was a proponent of religious freedom and played a role in the separation of church and state in Massachusetts.

418.

Paine was an early abolitionist and actively worked to end the institution of slavery.

419.

He was a founding member of the Massachusetts Society for Promoting Agriculture, demonstrating his interest in promoting agricultural innovation and productivity.

420.

Paine was a devoted family man and had nine children with his wife, Sally Cobb.

421.

After retiring from the bench, Paine devoted himself to writing and published several works on legal and political subjects.

422.

Paine's writings reflected his belief in the principles of liberty, justice, and individual rights.

423.

He was highly regarded for his legal acumen and was often consulted on important legal matters.

424.

Paine was known for his integrity, intelligence, and unwavering commitment to public service.

425.

He was a founding member of the American Academy of Arts and Sciences, a prestigious scholarly organization.

426.

Paine's contributions to the American Revolution and the early years of the United States earned him the respect and admiration of his contemporaries.

427.

He was described as a man of great intellect, kindness, and humility.

428.

Paine was an avid reader and lifelong learner, with a wide range of interests and knowledge.

429.

He had a deep appreciation for the arts and was a patron of literature and culture.

430.

Paine was deeply committed to the ideals of democracy and the pursuit of a just and equitable society.

431.

He believed in the power of education to transform individuals and society and advocated for universal access to education.

432.

Paine was a staunch defender of civil liberties and fought against any form of tyranny or oppression.

433.

He was known for his strong moral compass and his unwavering commitment to ethical conduct.

434.

Paine's contributions to the legal and political landscape of Massachusetts and the United States continue to be celebrated and remembered.

435.

His legacy lives on through his writings, legal decisions, and the principles he championed.

436.

Paine's dedication to public service and his commitment to the common good serve as an inspiration to future generations.

437.

He believed in the power of reason and the importance of dialogue and debate in shaping a just and prosperous society.

438.

Paine's intellectual contributions and legal expertise continue to be studied and appreciated by scholars and legal professionals.

439.

He was a man of strong convictions and was not afraid to speak out against injustice or advocate for unpopular causes.

440.

Paine's work laid the foundation for the development of American jurisprudence and legal theory.

441.

He was a key figure in the formation of the Massachusetts state constitution, which became a model for other states.

442.

Paine's commitment to public service extended beyond his political career, as he served as a volunteer firefighter in Taunton, Massachusetts.

443.

Paine was an early advocate for the protection of natural resources and played a role in the establishment of conservation policies.

444.

He was a strong supporter of the arts and culture, recognizing their importance in enriching society and fostering a sense of community.

445.

Paine's contributions to the American Revolution and the formation of the United States were recognized and celebrated during his lifetime.

446.

He was a man of great humility and did not seek personal glory or fame for his achievements.

447.

Paine believed in the power of democracy to bring about positive change and was an ardent defender of democratic principles.

448.

He was a firm believer in the separation of powers and checks and balances as essential elements of a functioning government.

449.

Paine's commitment to justice and equality made him a champion for the rights of all individuals, regardless of their social or economic status.

450.

Paine's life and work continue to inspire individuals to strive for a more just, inclusive, and democratic society.

451.

The Big Eyed Squirrel Fish (Myripristis sp.) is a species of marine fish found in tropical and subtropical waters.

452.

It gets its name from its large, protruding eyes, which give it an endearing and distinctive appearance.

453.

These fish can grow up to 6 to 10 inches in length, depending on the species.

454.

They have a vibrant coloration, with a reddish-orange body and yellow or orange fins.

455.

The Big Eyed Squirrel Fish is nocturnal, spending its days hiding in crevices or coral reefs and becoming active at night to hunt for food.

456.

They have sharp teeth that help them feed on small crustaceans, shrimp, and other small fish.

457.

These fish have a symbiotic relationship with cleaner shrimps, who help keep their bodies free from parasites by picking at their skin.

458.

Big Eyed Squirrel Fish are known for their ability to change coloration, adapting to their surroundings to blend in and hide from predators.

459.

They possess a specialized sensory system called the lateral line, which allows them to detect vibrations and movements in the water.

460.

These fish are generally solitary, although they may gather in small groups during mating season.

461.

Big Eyed Squirrel Fish have a unique reproductive strategy. Females release their eggs into the water column, and males fertilize them externally.

462.

The eggs hatch into larvae that spend several weeks floating in the ocean currents before settling into a reef environment.

463.

They are known for their strong swimming ability, using their pectoral fins to navigate through the water with precision.

464.

Big Eyed Squirrel Fish are found in various habitats, including coral reefs, rocky areas, and coastal lagoons.

465.

They are widespread in the Indo-Pacific region, including the Red Sea, Indian Ocean, and the Pacific Ocean.

466.

These fish are not typically targeted by commercial fisheries, but they can occasionally be found in the aquarium trade.

467.

Big Eyed Squirrel Fish are not considered endangered or threatened, as their populations are relatively stable.

468.

They are part of the family Holocentridae, which includes other species commonly known as squirrelfish.

469.

These fish have adapted to low-light conditions, thanks to their large eyes and specialized retina, which enhances their night vision.

470.

They are known to exhibit bioluminescent properties, with some species possessing light-producing organs on their bodies.

471.

Big Eyed Squirrel Fish use their bioluminescence as a form of communication and to attract prey.

472.

They are agile swimmers and can quickly change direction to evade predators or capture fast-moving prey.

473.

These fish have a lifespan of around 5 to 10 years in the wild.

474.

They are known to make clicking or grunting sounds, which they use to communicate with other members of their species.

475.

Big Eyed Squirrel Fish are territorial and will defend their preferred habitat from intruders.

476.

They have been observed displaying courtship behavior, including fin displays and head movements, during the mating season.

477.

The larvae of these fish are highly vulnerable to predation, and only a small percentage survive to adulthood.

478.

They are not considered a significant threat to humans and are generally not aggressive unless provoked.

479.

Big Eyed Squirrel Fish are known to exhibit schooling behavior when threatened, increasing their chances of survival.

480.

These fish have a remarkable ability to regenerate damaged or lost body parts, including fins.

481.

They have an elongated body shape, allowing them to navigate through narrow crevices and tight spaces in their habitat.

482.

Big Eyed Squirrel Fish are sensitive to changes in water temperature and quality, making them good indicators of environmental health.

483.

They have a specialized air bladder that helps them maintain buoyancy in the water.

484.

These fish have an excellent sense of smell, allowing them to detect food sources and potential predators.

485.

They are not known to migrate long distances but may move within their habitat in search of food or mates.

486.

Big Eyed Squirrel Fish have a high metabolic rate, requiring them to consume a significant amount of food to sustain their energy levels.

487.

They are often preyed upon by larger fish, including groupers, snappers, and barracudas.

488.

These fish have a unique mechanism called a "flicker fusion" that enables them to distinguish colors and patterns in low-light conditions.

489.

They are known to exhibit interesting behaviors, such as headstands and hovering, as they search for food.

490.

Big Eyed Squirrel Fish have a slender, streamlined body shape, allowing them to move through the water with minimal resistance.

491.

They have a strong jaw and sharp teeth, enabling them to capture and consume their prey efficiently.

492.

These fish have a relatively high tolerance for fluctuations in salinity and temperature, allowing them to inhabit diverse marine environments.

493.

They are typically more active during periods of high tide when prey availability is increased.

494.

Big Eyed Squirrel Fish have been studied for their bioluminescent properties, which could have applications in biotechnology and medical research.

495.

They are an integral part of the marine ecosystem, contributing to the balance of predator-prey relationships and nutrient cycling.

496.

These fish have a unique scale structure that provides protection and helps reduce drag as they swim through the water.

497.

They are known to exhibit courtship displays, including color changes and fin movements, to attract potential mates.

498.

Big Eyed Squirrel Fish have a complex visual system that allows them to detect subtle movements and changes in their environment.

499.

They are typically most active during the twilight hours, utilizing their excellent night vision to navigate and hunt for prey.

500.

These fish have a fascinating reproductive cycle, with distinct stages of larval development and gradual metamorphosis into adults.

501.

The Bigfin Reef Squid (Sepioteuthis lessoniana) is a species of cephalopod found in warm coastal waters of the Indo-Pacific region.

502.

It gets its name from its distinctive elongated fins, which are proportionally larger than those of other squid species.

503.

These squids can reach a length of up to 40 centimeters (16 inches), making them relatively large compared to other reef-dwelling squid.

504.

Bigfin Reef Squids have a slender, cylindrical body shape, allowing them to navigate through coral reefs and other marine habitats with ease.

505.

They have a soft, gelatinous body covered in chromatophores, specialized cells that allow them to change color and pattern for camouflage and communication.

506.

These squids exhibit a wide range of colors, including various shades of brown, red, yellow, and white, enabling them to blend into their surroundings.

507.

Bigfin Reef Squids are highly adaptable and can be found in various coastal environments, including coral reefs, mangroves, and seagrass beds.

508.

They are swift swimmers, using jet propulsion to move through the water by expelling water from a muscular funnel.

509.

These squids are skilled hunters, feeding primarily on small fish, crustaceans, and other mollusks.

510.

Bigfin Reef Squids use their tentacles, equipped with suckers and hooks, to capture and subdue their prey.

511.

They have well-developed eyes and excellent vision, allowing them to detect movements and prey items from a distance.

512.

These squids possess a beak-like mouthpart called a buccal mass, which they use to crush and consume their prey.

513.

Bigfin Reef Squids are known to exhibit complex social behaviors, forming schools or aggregations of individuals for protection and mating purposes.

514.

Within schools, they communicate using visual displays, changes in body coloration, and rapid, coordinated movements.

515.

Mating in Bigfin Reef Squids involves a unique courtship display, with males performing intricate swimming patterns and color changes to attract females.

516.

After mating, females lay eggs in clusters or strings, which are attached to rocky substrates or vegetation in the water.

517.

The eggs are protected by a gelatinous casing, and the female guards and cares for them until they hatch.

518.

Bigfin Reef Squid larvae undergo a planktonic stage, drifting in the ocean currents until they develop into juveniles and settle in coastal areas.

519.

They have a relatively short lifespan, typically living for about one year.

520.

These squids have a remarkable ability to regenerate lost or damaged body parts, including tentacles and fins.

521.

Bigfin Reef Squids have been studied for their complex nervous system and intelligence, demonstrating problem-solving and learning abilities.

522.

They are capable of rapid color changes and pattern displays as a means of communication, including during confrontations with predators or rivals.

523.

These squids are preyed upon by various marine predators, including larger fish, sea birds, and marine mammals.

524.

They have several defense mechanisms, including ink release to create a cloud and confuse predators, as well as jet propulsion to escape quickly.

525.

Bigfin Reef Squids are not typically targeted by commercial fisheries but may be caught incidentally in fishing nets.

526.

They are considered an important part of the marine food chain, serving as both predator and prey.

527.

These squids have been the subject of scientific research to understand their behavior, physiology, and ecological role.

528.

Bigfin Reef Squids are known to exhibit both diurnal and nocturnal activity patterns, depending on factors such as predation risk and food availability.

529.

They have a high metabolism and require a consistent intake of food to sustain their energy levels.

530.

These squids have a complex reproductive system, with separate sexes and internal fertilization.

531.

They are capable of producing large numbers of eggs during each reproductive cycle to ensure the survival of their species.

532.

Bigfin Reef Squids have a well-developed nervous system, with a large brain and specialized ganglia that control their movement and behavior.

533.

They are highly sensitive to changes in water temperature and salinity, as well as other environmental factors.

534.

These squids are known to exhibit a phenomenon called "tidal vertical migration," where they move up and down in the water column in response to tidal cycles.

535.

Bigfin Reef Squids have been observed engaging in "flashing" behavior, where they produce brief bursts of light using specialized light-emitting cells called photophores.

536.

They are considered an important indicator species for the health of coral reef ecosystems, as their presence or absence can reflect the overall ecosystem condition.

537.

These squids have a unique ability to camouflage themselves by adjusting their skin texture and color to match their surroundings.

538.

They have been known to display cooperative hunting behavior, with individuals working together to capture larger prey.

539.

Bigfin Reef Squids have large eyes relative to their body size, providing them with excellent depth perception and the ability to see in low-light conditions.

540.

These squids are highly sensitive to changes in water pressure, allowing them to navigate in different water depths.

541.

They possess a complex digestive system, including a muscular stomach and a long digestive tract for efficient nutrient absorption.

542.

Bigfin Reef Squids have been studied for their bioluminescent properties, with scientists exploring their potential use in medical and technological applications.

543.

They are highly skilled at evading predators through rapid changes in direction, speed, and camouflage.

544.

These squids have been observed engaging in territorial behaviors, defending their preferred habitat or mating sites.

545.

They have the ability to regenerate lost tissue, including parts of their mantle and tentacles.

546.

Bigfin Reef Squids are known to exhibit cephalopod behaviors such as "jetting," where they rapidly expel water to create propulsion.

547.

They have a complex circulatory system, with three hearts that pump blood throughout their body.

548.

These squids can detect changes in water pressure and vibrations using specialized sensory organs called statocysts.

549.

They have a remarkable ability to squeeze through small openings and crevices, allowing them to hide from predators or escape confined spaces.

550.

Bigfin Reef Squids are a fascinating and ecologically important species, contributing to the biodiversity and balance of marine ecosystems in the Indo-Pacific region.

551.

The Lehner Mammoth-Kill Site is an archaeological site located in Arizona, United States.

552.

It was discovered in 1952 by Emil Haury, a prominent American archaeologist.

553.

The site is named after Frank Lehner, a local rancher who owned the land where the site is located.

554.

The Lehner Mammoth-Kill Site is one of the earliest known archaeological sites in North America, dating back approximately 10,000 years.

555.

It provides important evidence of early human activity in the region and offers insights into the hunting practices of ancient peoples.

556.

The site is associated with the Clovis culture, a prehistoric Paleo-Indian culture known for their distinctive stone tools.

557.

Archaeological excavations at the site have revealed numerous mammoth bones, indicating that mammoths were the primary target of the hunters.

558.

The mammoth bones found at the site show evidence of butchering and tool marks, suggesting that the ancient hunters used spears and other weapons to kill and process the animals.

559.

In addition to mammoth bones, the site has also yielded the remains of other extinct animals, including bison, camelids, and horses.

560.

The presence of these large herbivores suggests that the area was once a grassland or savannah environment.

561.

The Lehner Mammoth-Kill Site has provided important information about the diet and subsistence strategies of early humans in the region.

562.

The site is located near the San Pedro River, which would have provided a water source for the ancient hunters and their prey.

563.

The archaeological remains found at the site indicate that it was likely a temporary hunting camp used by mobile groups of early humans.

564.

The discovery of stone tools and projectile points suggests that the hunters were skilled in crafting weapons for hunting purposes.

565.

The Lehner Mammoth-Kill Site has been studied extensively by archaeologists, who have used various scientific techniques to analyze the artifacts and bones.

566.

Radiocarbon dating has been used to establish the age of the site and the remains found within it.

567.

The site has also provided evidence of early human use of fire, as charred bone fragments and hearths have been discovered.

568.

The archaeological findings at the Lehner Mammoth-Kill Site have contributed to our understanding of the peopling of the Americas and

the interactions between humans and megafauna during the
Pleistocene era.

569.

The site is part of the broader archaeological landscape of the
Southwest United States, which contains numerous sites of cultural
and historical significance.

570.

Excavations at the Lehner Mammoth-Kill Site have involved
meticulous documentation and careful preservation of the artifacts
and bones found.

571.

The site has been a subject of ongoing research, with new
discoveries and interpretations continuing to contribute to our
knowledge of prehistoric human life in North America.

572.

The Lehner Mammoth-Kill Site is an important educational
resource, providing opportunities for students and researchers to
learn about archaeology and ancient human cultures.

573.

The site has been designated as a National Historic Landmark,
recognizing its significance in American history and archaeology.

574.

The Lehner Mammoth-Kill Site offers visitors the chance to see a
reconstructed representation of the ancient hunting scene and learn
about the techniques and tools used by early hunters.

575.

The site is surrounded by a natural landscape, allowing visitors to appreciate the environment in which the ancient hunters lived and hunted.

576.

Excavations at the site have revealed evidence of other cultural activities, such as the manufacture of stone tools and the presence of hearths for cooking and warmth.

577.

The archaeological record at the Lehner Mammoth-Kill Site provides a glimpse into the lifeways and adaptations of early humans in the Southwest region.

578.

The site has yielded a wealth of data that has helped archaeologists understand the timing and nature of the extinction of megafauna in North America.

579.

The discovery of stone tools and other artifacts at the site has shed light on the technological advancements of early human societies.

580.

The Lehner Mammoth-Kill Site is an example of the collaborative efforts between archaeologists, landowners, and local communities to preserve and study archaeological heritage.

581.

The site has inspired further research and exploration into the early human history of the Americas.

582.

The Lehner Mammoth-Kill Site serves as a reminder of the ancient connection between humans and the natural world, and the role of hunting in early societies.

583.

The presence of mammoth bones at the site indicates that the ancient hunters were able to successfully take down these massive animals, demonstrating their resourcefulness and hunting skills.

584.

The site provides a window into the past, offering insights into the cultural, technological, and ecological aspects of early human life in North America.

585.

The artifacts and remains found at the Lehner Mammoth-Kill Site have been carefully studied and analyzed to reconstruct the paleoenvironment and understand the interactions between humans and the animal species of the time.

586.

Excavations at the site have uncovered evidence of the processing and utilization of animal resources, such as bone tools and evidence of bone marrow extraction.

587.

The site has yielded a diverse range of artifacts, including stone projectile points, scrapers, and other tools that were used for various purposes.

588.

Analysis of the archaeological remains has provided insights into the social organization and mobility patterns of the ancient hunters.

589.

The Lehner Mammoth-Kill Site has served as a catalyst for interdisciplinary research, bringing together experts from fields such as archaeology, paleontology, geology, and environmental science.

590.

The preservation of the site has involved careful documentation, mapping, and protection of the archaeological features and artifacts.

591.

The Lehner Mammoth-Kill Site has contributed to our understanding of the timeline and processes of human migration into the Americas.

592.

The site has been compared to other similar archaeological sites across North America, allowing for comparative studies and a broader understanding of prehistoric human activities.

593.

The presence of hearths and fire-related features at the site has provided insights into the use of fire for cooking, warmth, and tool production.

594.

The site has revealed evidence of tool manufacturing and maintenance, suggesting a sophisticated understanding of lithic technology by the ancient inhabitants.

595.

The discovery of perishable artifacts, such as wooden tools or textiles, could provide additional insights into the material culture of the ancient hunters, although such artifacts are rare due to the passage of time.

596.

The Lehner Mammoth-Kill Site has been a focus of ongoing
scientific inquiry, with new techniques and methods being applied to
the existing collections to gain fresh insights into the site.

597.

The site has been visited by scholars, students, and the general
public, offering opportunities for education and interpretation of the
archaeological record.

598.

The Lehner Mammoth-Kill Site is a testament to the endurance of
archaeological materials over thousands of years and the dedication
of researchers in piecing together the puzzle of the past.

599.

The site has provided valuable data on the ecological conditions and
climate of the region during the time of the ancient hunters.

600.

The Lehner Mammoth-Kill Site continues to be a site of significance
and inspiration for ongoing research into the prehistoric cultures and
environments of the American Southwest.

601.

Los Santos Ángeles de Guevavi is a historic mission site located in
southern Arizona, United States.

602.

The site was established in 1691 by the Jesuit missionary Eusebio
Francisco Kino.

603.

It was one of the first Spanish missions in Arizona and played a
significant role in the Spanish colonization of the region.

604.

The mission was built to serve the O'odham (Pima) and Apache indigenous communities.

605.

The name "Los Santos Ángeles de Guevavi" translates to "The Holy Angels of Guevavi."

606.

Guevavi was the name of the nearby O'odham village where the mission was located.

607.

The mission was initially a simple adobe structure, but it was later expanded and fortified.

608.

It served as a center for religious activities, education, and agriculture for the indigenous populations.

609.

The mission complex included a church, living quarters for the priests, workshops, gardens, and defensive walls.

610.

The church at Guevavi was known for its beautiful architecture and artwork, including frescoes and sculptures.

611.

The mission faced numerous challenges, including conflicts with the Apache tribes and the scarcity of resources in the arid region.

612.

Despite these challenges, the mission thrived for several decades, attracting indigenous converts and establishing a strong presence in the area.

613.

Guevavi was part of a network of missions established by the Spanish in the Southwest, known as the Jesuit Missions of the Pimería Alta.

614.

In 1767, the Jesuits were expelled from the Spanish colonies, and the Franciscans took over the mission at Guevavi.

615.

The mission declined in the late 18th century due to Apache raids, disease, and political changes in the region.

616.

By the early 19th century, the mission was abandoned, and the remaining structures fell into ruin.

617.

The ruins of Guevavi were rediscovered in the 20th century, and efforts were made to preserve and study the site.

618.

Archaeological excavations have revealed artifacts and remnants of the mission complex, providing insights into the daily life and activities of the mission community.

619.

The site is now part of the Tumacácori National Historical Park, managed by the National Park Service.

620.

Visitors to Los Santos Ángeles de Guevavi can explore the ruins and learn about the history and cultural significance of the mission.

621.

Interpretive signs and exhibits provide information about the mission's architecture, religious practices, and interactions with indigenous communities.

622.

The mission site offers a serene and picturesque setting, surrounded by desert landscapes and scenic views of the Santa Cruz River Valley.

623.

Los Santos Ángeles de Guevavi is a designated National Historic Landmark, recognizing its importance in American history.

624.

The mission's location in southern Arizona reflects the broader history of Spanish colonization and the interaction between European colonizers and indigenous peoples.

625.

The mission's architecture blends European and indigenous styles, representing a fusion of cultural influences.

626.

Guevavi and the other missions of the Pimería Alta played a significant role in spreading Christianity and European culture among the indigenous populations of the Southwest.

627.

The mission was not only a religious institution but also a center for trade, agriculture, and education.

628.

The agricultural activities of the mission included the cultivation of crops such as wheat, corn, and beans, as well as the raising of livestock.

629.

The mission community was self-sufficient, producing much of its own food, clothing, and other necessities.

630.

The mission priests served as intermediaries between the indigenous communities and the Spanish colonial authorities, playing a crucial role in maintaining order and facilitating communication.

631.

The mission complex at Guevavi was designed to be both functional and symbolic, with the church serving as the focal point of the community.

632.

The religious ceremonies and rituals conducted at the mission incorporated elements of both Spanish Catholicism and indigenous beliefs.

633.

Guevavi and the other missions in the region faced challenges in converting indigenous peoples to Christianity, as many held strong cultural and spiritual traditions.

634.

The mission system in the Southwest had both positive and negative impacts on indigenous communities, including changes in lifestyle, loss of land, and disruptions to traditional practices.

635.

The mission era in the Southwest came to an end with Mexican independence from Spain in the early 19th century, which led to the secularization of the missions.

636.

The ruins of Guevavi provide a tangible connection to the complex and layered history of the region, serving as a reminder of the interactions and conflicts between different cultures.

637.

The preservation and interpretation of Guevavi and other mission sites contribute to a deeper understanding of the diverse heritage and historical experiences of the Southwest.

638.

The mission site has attracted researchers and scholars from various disciplines, including archaeology, history, anthropology, and religious studies.

639.

Excavations and studies at Guevavi have revealed insights into the daily lives of both the missionaries and the indigenous peoples who inhabited the mission.

640.

The mission complex at Guevavi was part of a larger network of Spanish colonial settlements and outposts that extended throughout the Southwest and beyond.

641.

The mission system in the Southwest was influenced by the Spanish desire for political control, economic exploitation, and the spread of Christianity.

642.

The ruins of Guevavi are a testament to the resilience and adaptability of the indigenous communities who lived in the area and navigated the challenges posed by colonialism.

643.

The mission's decline and abandonment reflect larger historical trends, including changing political dynamics and the impact of diseases brought by European colonizers.

644.

Guevavi's location in the Santa Cruz River Valley provided access to water and fertile land, making it an attractive site for settlement and agriculture.

645.

The mission complex at Guevavi was constructed using local materials, such as adobe bricks made from the surrounding clay soil.

646.

The mission community included not only priests and indigenous converts but also Spanish soldiers, craftsmen, and settlers who supported the mission's activities.

647.

Guevavi and the other missions of the Pimería Alta were part of a broader system of colonial control and influence, aimed at securing Spanish claims to the region and converting indigenous peoples.

648.

The legacy of Guevavi and the mission era in the Southwest continues to be explored and interpreted by contemporary scholars, educators, and indigenous communities.

649.

The ruins of Guevavi offer a tangible link to the past, allowing visitors to connect with the people and events that shaped the history of the region.

650.

The preservation and interpretation of Guevavi contribute to the ongoing dialogue about colonialism, cultural heritage, and the legacies of the past in the present.

651.

Francis Daniel Pastorius was a German immigrant who played a significant role in the establishment of Germantown, Pennsylvania, in the late 17th century.

652.

He was born on September 26, 1651, in Sommerhausen, Germany, and belonged to a prominent family.

653.

Pastorius studied law at the University of Altdorf and became a lawyer before emigrating to America.

654.

In 1683, Pastorius led a group of 13 families to settle in the area that would become Germantown, making him one of the founders of the town.

655.

He is often referred to as the "Father of Germantown" due to his leadership and influence in the early development of the community.

656.

Pastorius was a Quaker and actively promoted the principles of peace, equality, and religious tolerance in Germantown.

657.

He drafted the Germantown Protest in 1688, which was one of the earliest documented protests against slavery in the American colonies.

658.

The Germantown Protest, also known as the "Germantown Quaker Petition Against Slavery," expressed Quaker concerns about the morality and injustice of slavery.

659.

Pastorius advocated for the fair treatment of Native Americans and established positive relations with the Lenape people in the region.

660.

He authored several works, including "The Bee-Hive," a collection of maxims and aphorisms promoting moral and ethical behavior.

661.

As a lawyer, Pastorius played a crucial role in mediating disputes and providing legal counsel to the residents of Germantown.

662.

He was known for his intellectual pursuits and love of literature, poetry, and philosophy.

663.

Pastorius corresponded with prominent thinkers of his time, including William Penn and John Locke.

664.

He founded the first public school in Germantown, known as the Germantown Academy, to provide education to the community's children.

665.

Pastorius was a skilled linguist and translated many works from Latin, Greek, and Dutch into English.

666.

He had a deep interest in botany and horticulture and cultivated a variety of plants in Germantown.

667.

Pastorius encouraged the establishment of small industries and businesses in Germantown, contributing to its economic growth.

668.

He wrote a letter to William Penn in 1684 proposing the establishment of a colonial assembly in Pennsylvania, advocating for self-governance.

669.

Pastorius was involved in land acquisition and helped negotiate treaties with Native American tribes to ensure peaceful coexistence.

670.

He was appointed as a judge in Germantown and served as a representative in the Pennsylvania Provincial Council.

671.

Pastorius was a strong advocate for women's rights and believed in the equality of men and women.

672.

He married Ennecke Klostermann in 1675, and they had six children together.

673.

Pastorius was known for his strong moral character, integrity, and dedication to his community.

674.

He maintained a diary in which he recorded his daily activities, thoughts, and observations, providing valuable insights into colonial life.

675.

Pastorius participated in the founding of the Free Society of Traders, a trading company that aimed to promote economic development in Pennsylvania.

676.

He made significant contributions to the development of German literature in America and is considered one of the pioneers of German-American literature.

677.

Pastorius promoted the use of the German language in education and religious practices in Germantown.

678.

He compiled a legal handbook titled "A Pocket Almanack," which served as a guide to Pennsylvania law for colonists.

679.

Pastorius actively participated in religious life in Germantown and helped establish the first German-speaking Mennonite congregation in the region.

680.

He believed in the importance of community service and worked to improve public infrastructure in Germantown, including road construction and maintenance.

681.

Pastorius had a passion for urban planning and envisioned Germantown as a well-designed and organized town with clearly defined lots and streets.

682.

He was instrumental in the establishment of Germantown's first library, which provided access to books and knowledge for the community.

683.

Pastorius was a proponent of scientific inquiry and supported scientific experiments and observations within the community.

684.

He was a skilled calligrapher and created beautifully decorated manuscripts.

685.

Pastorius had a deep appreciation for nature and advocated for the preservation of natural landscapes in and around Germantown.

686.

He participated in the founding of the first German-language printing press in America, which helped disseminate German literature and culture.

687.

Pastorius was committed to social justice and worked to ensure fair treatment for all residents of Germantown, regardless of their social or economic status.

688.

He believed in the power of education to uplift individuals and society and actively promoted educational opportunities for all.

689.

Pastorius corresponded with other German immigrants, encouraging them to settle in Germantown and contribute to its growth.

690.

He was an early advocate for religious freedom and the separation of church and state.

691.

Pastorius played a key role in the development of Germantown's agricultural sector, promoting innovative farming practices and crop diversification.

692.

He encouraged the establishment of trade relationships between Germantown and other communities, fostering economic growth and cultural exchange.

693.

Pastorius was known for his wit and sense of humor, often using satire and irony in his writings.

694.

He believed in the importance of self-discipline and self-improvement, advocating for personal virtues such as honesty, humility, and temperance.

695.

Pastorius maintained strong connections with his German heritage and sought to preserve and promote German culture in America.

696.

He was involved in the planning and construction of Germantown's first public market, providing a central space for commerce and trade.

697.

Pastorius's efforts to promote the welfare and prosperity of Germantown earned him the respect and admiration of his fellow colonists.

698.

He was a firm believer in democratic principles and actively participated in local governance, advocating for the rights and interests of the community.

699.

Pastorius's writings and ideas had a lasting impact on the development of Pennsylvania and the broader American society.

700.

His legacy as a visionary leader, scholar, and advocate for justice and equality continues to inspire and resonate in Germantown and beyond.

701.

The Bigfin Squid, scientifically known as Magnapinna sp., is a deep-sea cephalopod that belongs to the family Magnapinnidae.

702.

They are commonly referred to as "Bigfin Squid" due to their exceptionally long and slender fins.

703.

Bigfin Squid are typically found in the mesopelagic and bathypelagic zones of the ocean, which can range from 200 meters to over 4,000 meters deep.

704.

They have a unique body shape, characterized by elongated arms and tentacles and a small mantle.

705.

Bigfin Squid are one of the most enigmatic and rarely seen cephalopods, making their behavior and ecology poorly understood.

706.

Their elongated fins can reach lengths that are several times the length of their body, giving them a distinct appearance.

707.

The exact purpose of the Bigfin Squid's large fins is still unknown, but it is speculated that they aid in stability and maneuverability in deep-sea environments.

708.

They possess large, complex eyes, allowing them to detect bioluminescent signals and navigate in low-light conditions.

709.

The arms and tentacles of the Bigfin Squid are equipped with rows of small hooks, which they use to capture and secure their prey.

710.

Their diet mainly consists of small fish, crustaceans, and other cephalopods.

711.

Bigfin Squid are known to display bioluminescent properties, producing light from their bodies to communicate and attract prey or potential mates.

712.

These cephalopods have been observed exhibiting a unique hovering behavior, where they remain motionless in the water column, possibly using their fins for stability.

713.

The reproductive behavior of Bigfin Squid is largely unknown, but it is believed that they have a short lifespan and reproduce relatively quickly.

714.

The size of Bigfin Squid can vary greatly, with some individuals measuring only a few centimeters in length, while others can reach several meters long.

715.

Due to their elusive nature and deep-sea habitat, the majority of information about Bigfin Squid comes from rare sightings and specimens caught in fishing nets or trawls.

716.

They are found in oceans worldwide, although their distribution is patchy and influenced by oceanographic conditions.

717.

Bigfin Squid have been observed in various regions, including the Atlantic, Pacific, and Indian Oceans.

718.

The first recorded sighting of a Bigfin Squid was in 1988 off the coast of Brazil, captured by a remotely operated vehicle (ROV) during a deep-sea exploration mission.

719.

Their translucent appearance allows them to blend into their deep-sea surroundings, making them difficult to spot.

720.

Bigfin Squid are not known to be aggressive towards humans and are not considered a threat.

721.

They have a soft and gelatinous body, making them delicate and vulnerable to damage during capture or collection.

722.

The taxonomy and classification of Bigfin Squid are still a subject of debate among scientists, with ongoing research to determine the exact species and relationships within the genus.

723.

They are believed to have evolved specialized adaptations to survive in the extreme conditions of the deep sea, including low temperatures, high pressures, and limited food resources.

724.

Bigfin Squid are often encountered in deep-sea expeditions or trawl surveys, providing valuable insights into their distribution and behavior.

725.

The study of Bigfin Squid is challenging due to their fragile nature and the difficulties of conducting research in deep-sea environments.

726.

Scientists rely on technological advancements, such as underwater vehicles and deep-sea cameras, to capture images and footage of Bigfin Squid in their natural habitat.

727.

Bigfin Squid are known to exhibit vertical migration patterns, moving between different depths of the ocean in search of prey and favorable conditions.

728.

Their ability to adjust their body position and posture in the water column allows them to optimize their foraging and feeding strategies.

729.

Bigfin Squid are believed to have a relatively low metabolic rate, allowing them to conserve energy in the deep-sea environment where food resources are scarce.

730.

They are considered an important part of the deep-sea ecosystem, contributing to the food web and serving as prey for larger predators.

731.

Bigfin Squid are often encountered alongside other deep-sea organisms, such as deep-sea fish, jellyfish, and other cephalopods.

732.

The coloration of Bigfin Squid is generally light or translucent, allowing them to camouflage and avoid detection by predators.

733.

Some species of Bigfin Squid exhibit sexual dimorphism, with males and females differing in size and morphology.

734.

They possess a complex nervous system, allowing them to process sensory information and exhibit coordinated movements.

735.

The exact lifespan of Bigfin Squid is unknown, but it is believed to be relatively short due to the harsh conditions of their deep-sea habitat.

736.

Their fins are supported by a unique cartilaginous structure, providing flexibility and maneuverability.

737.

Bigfin Squid are often encountered in deep-sea canyons and seamounts, where upwelling currents bring nutrients and attract a variety of marine life.

738.

They are believed to be opportunistic predators, feeding on available prey items and adjusting their diet based on local abundance.

739.

The population dynamics and abundance of Bigfin Squid are difficult to assess due to their sporadic occurrence and the challenges of studying deep-sea ecosystems.

740.

Their presence in different oceanic regions suggests some level of dispersal and migration, although the mechanisms and patterns are not well understood.

741.

Bigfin Squid have been the subject of artistic representation and inspiration, appearing in various forms of media and literature depicting the mysteries of the deep sea.

742.

They are part of a larger group of deep-sea cephalopods, collectively known as "deep-sea squids," which exhibit unique adaptations to survive in extreme environments.

743.

The discovery and study of Bigfin Squid contribute to our understanding of the biodiversity and ecological dynamics of the deep sea, which remains one of the least explored regions on Earth.

744.

The reproductive strategies of Bigfin Squid, including mating behavior, spawning, and the development of their offspring, are still largely unknown.

745.

They are believed to have a relatively fast growth rate, allowing them to reach sexual maturity at a young age and maximize their reproductive potential.

746.

Bigfin Squid possess chromatophores, specialized cells in their skin that can change color and pattern, potentially used for communication and camouflage.

747.

Their long, thin fins have a flexible and wavy appearance, resembling ribbons or streamers as they undulate in the water.

748.

The behavior of Bigfin Squid in their natural habitat is mostly speculative, as direct observations are rare and limited.

749.

Their unique morphology and adaptations have fascinated scientists and researchers, spurring further investigation into the biology and ecology of deep-sea cephalopods.

750.

Bigfin Squid serve as a reminder of the incredible diversity and adaptations found in the vast depths of our oceans, highlighting the need for conservation and protection of these fragile and poorly understood ecosystems.

751.

The Black Caiman, scientific name Melanosuchus niger, is the largest species of caiman and one of the largest reptiles in the Americas.

752.

They are primarily found in the rivers, swamps, and lakes of South America, including the Amazon Basin and the Orinoco River.

753.

Black Caimans have a distinctive black coloration, which helps them blend into their aquatic environments and provides camouflage.

754.

They have a robust body with a broad head and strong jaws, equipped with numerous sharp teeth.

755.

Adult males can reach lengths of up to 5 meters (16 feet) and weigh over 400 kilograms (880 pounds), making them a formidable predator.

756.

The average lifespan of Black Caimans in the wild is estimated to be around 50-60 years.

757.

They are well adapted to an aquatic lifestyle and are excellent swimmers, using their powerful tails to propel themselves through the water.

758.

Black Caimans are opportunistic carnivores, feeding on a variety of prey, including fish, birds, reptiles, mammals, and even large invertebrates.

759.

They are ambush predators, patiently waiting for prey to come within striking distance before launching a swift attack.

760.

Black Caimans have a remarkable ability to hold their breath underwater for extended periods, thanks to their efficient respiratory system and the ability to slow their heart rate.

761.

They possess a specialized transparent third eyelid called a
nictitating membrane, which helps protect their eyes while
underwater.

762.

Breeding occurs during the wet season, and female Black Caimans
construct large nests made of vegetation, where they lay their eggs.

763.

The female fiercely guards the nest, protecting it from potential
predators until the hatchlings emerge.

764.

The sex of the hatchlings is determined by the temperature at which
the eggs are incubated, with higher temperatures producing males
and lower temperatures producing females.

765.

The young caimans are highly vulnerable to predation, and only a
small percentage will survive to adulthood.

766.

Black Caimans play an important role in their ecosystems as top
predators, helping to regulate populations of their prey species.

767.

They are known to display territorial behavior, defending their
preferred hunting grounds and nesting sites from intruders.

768.

Black Caimans have been hunted for their skins, which are highly
valued in the luxury leather industry. This, combined with habitat
loss, has resulted in population declines in some areas.

769.

Conservation efforts are in place to protect Black Caimans, including establishing protected areas and implementing sustainable hunting practices.

770.

Their large size and reputation as apex predators have made them the subject of folklore and legends among indigenous communities in South America.

771.

Black Caimans have a unique reproductive strategy known as facultative parental care, where the mother provides protection and care for her offspring, even after they hatch.

772.

They have a powerful bite force, capable of exerting tremendous pressure, which helps them immobilize and subdue their prey.

773.

Black Caimans have a keen sense of hearing and can detect sounds and vibrations in the water, allowing them to locate potential prey.

774.

They are more active during the night, using their excellent night vision to navigate and hunt.

775.

Black Caimans have been observed using lures to attract prey. They will balance sticks or branches on their heads and wait for curious birds to investigate, then quickly strike.

776.

They are known to exhibit basking behavior, sunning themselves on riverbanks or logs to regulate their body temperature.

777.

Black Caimans have a complex social structure and can form small groups or aggregations, particularly during the breeding season.

778.

Their rough, scaly skin provides protection from abrasions and helps reduce drag when swimming.

779.

Black Caimans have a unique gland called the "scute gland" on their tails, which produces a musky odor believed to play a role in communication.

780.

They have been observed engaging in "water dancing," where they perform a series of rapid head and tail movements on the surface of the water, possibly as a territorial display or courtship behavior.

781.

The Black Caiman has been listed as a vulnerable species by the International Union for Conservation of Nature (IUCN) due to habitat loss, hunting, and pollution.

782.

They are considered a flagship species for conservation efforts in the Amazon rainforest, as their protection helps preserve the overall health and biodiversity of the ecosystem.

783.

Black Caimans are capable of regenerating damaged or lost teeth throughout their lifetime, ensuring their hunting efficiency is not compromised.

784.

Their eyes have a reflective layer called the tapetum lucidum, which enhances their vision in low-light conditions.

785.

Black Caimans play a vital role in nutrient cycling, as their feces contribute to the nutrient enrichment of aquatic ecosystems, benefiting plant and algae growth.

786.

They have a powerful immune system that allows them to resist infections and heal wounds quickly, minimizing the risk of bacterial or fungal infections in their aquatic environment.

787.

Black Caimans have been studied for their remarkable ability to detect and interpret subtle changes in water pressure, allowing them to locate prey even in murky or turbid conditions.

788.

They are known to form mutualistic relationships with certain bird species, such as the yellow-billed tern, where the birds feed on insects and parasites found on the caiman's skin.

789.

Black Caimans have a unique vocal repertoire, communicating through various vocalizations, including hissing, grunting, and bellowing.

790.

They have a specialized gland called the "parietal eye," located on the top of their heads, which is sensitive to changes in light and helps them detect predators from above.

791.

Black Caimans are excellent climbers and can scale vertical riverbanks and vegetation using their strong limbs and claws.

792.

They have a remarkable ability to regenerate damaged or lost scales, ensuring the integrity and protection of their skin.

793.

Black Caimans have been observed engaging in group feeding behavior, where several individuals cooperate to corral and capture schools of fish.

794.

They are known to exhibit territorial displays, such as snout-arching, head-slapping, and bubble-blowing, to establish dominance and defend their territory.

795.

Black Caimans have been observed using their tails as weapons, delivering powerful strikes to potential threats or rivals.

796.

They have a unique circulatory system that helps them conserve heat in cold water and dissipate heat in warm environments, allowing them to maintain their body temperature within a narrow range.

797.

Black Caimans have a remarkable ability to recover from injuries and wounds, thanks to their efficient blood clotting mechanisms and rapid tissue regeneration.

798.

They are considered a keystone species in their habitats, as their presence and activities have far-reaching effects on the structure and functioning of the ecosystem.

799.

Black Caimans have been the subject of scientific research and conservation programs aimed at understanding their behavior, ecology, and population dynamics.

800.

Their formidable appearance and role as top predators make Black Caimans an iconic symbol of the Amazon rainforest, captivating the imagination of wildlife enthusiasts and researchers alike.

801.

Lowell Observatory is an astronomical observatory located in Flagstaff, Arizona, USA.

802.

It was founded in 1894 by astronomer Percival Lowell.

803.

The observatory's primary focus is on astronomical research, including planetary science, stellar astrophysics, and cosmology.

804.

Lowell Observatory is known for its pioneering work in the study of Mars. Percival Lowell conducted extensive observations of the planet, mapping its surface features and hypothesizing the existence of canals.

805.

The observatory's most famous telescope is the Clark Refractor, a 24-inch (61 cm) refracting telescope that is still in use today.

806.

The Clark Refractor was used to discover Pluto in 1930 by astronomer Clyde Tombaugh. It remained the largest telescope used for planetary research until the mid-20th century.

807.

Lowell Observatory is also known for its research on the outer solar system. Astronomer Gerard Kuiper discovered the existence of the Kuiper Belt, a region beyond Neptune populated by small icy bodies.

808.

The observatory's Mars Hill campus, where the main telescopes are located, sits at an elevation of 7,200 feet (2,200 meters), providing excellent viewing conditions for astronomical observations.

809.

Lowell Observatory has played a significant role in the study of asteroids. In 1912, astronomer Vesto Melvin Slipher discovered that the majority of asteroids have a reddish color.

810.

The observatory's research also includes studying variable stars, supernovae, and the formation and evolution of galaxies.

811.

Lowell Observatory operates the Discovery Channel Telescope, a 4.3-meter (14-foot) telescope located in Happy Jack, Arizona. It is used for a wide range of astronomical research projects.

812.

The observatory offers public programs and tours, allowing visitors to explore the facilities and learn about astronomy. It hosts stargazing events and provides opportunities to view celestial objects through telescopes.

813.

Percival Lowell's vision for the observatory was to conduct serious astronomical research while also engaging the public and promoting the study of science.

814.

Lowell Observatory has a long history of collaboration with NASA. It has provided support for various NASA missions, including the Mars Pathfinder mission and the New Horizons mission to Pluto.

815.

The observatory has a strong commitment to education and outreach. It offers educational programs for students of all ages, including workshops, summer camps, and teacher training.

816.

In 1994, Lowell Observatory celebrated its centennial, marking a hundred years of astronomical discoveries and advancements in scientific research.

817.

The observatory's research facilities include multiple telescopes, including the 72-inch Perkins Telescope, the 42-inch Hall Telescope, and the 31-inch John S. Hall Telescope.

818.

Lowell Observatory played a crucial role in the development of modern astrophotography techniques. Astronomer V.M. Slipher was one of the first to use spectroscopy to study celestial objects, revealing valuable information about their composition and motion.

819.

The observatory's historic Rotunda Museum houses exhibits on the history of astronomy, including artifacts and photographs related to the observatory's discoveries.

820.

Lowell Observatory's astronomers have made significant contributions to the study of comets, including the discovery and characterization of several comets.

821.

In 2001, Lowell Observatory became a founding partner of the United States Naval Observatory's Flagstaff Station, collaborating on various astronomical research projects.

822.

The observatory has an extensive collection of astronomical photographs, spanning over a century of observations. These photographs provide valuable data for studying long-term changes in celestial objects.

823.

Lowell Observatory has been involved in the search for exoplanets, including participating in the Kepler mission, which aimed to discover planets beyond our solar system.

824.

The observatory has a long-standing commitment to public outreach and science education, hosting numerous events, lectures, and workshops for the general public and schools.

825.

Lowell Observatory offers opportunities for amateur astronomers to conduct research and contribute to scientific discoveries through its Lowell Amateur Research Initiative (LARI) program.

826.

The observatory's Dark Sky Initiative promotes awareness of light pollution and advocates for responsible outdoor lighting practices to preserve the dark skies of Flagstaff.

827.

Lowell Observatory has a library and archives that contain a wealth of historical documents, manuscripts, and photographs related to the history of astronomy.

828.

The observatory's staff includes professional astronomers, educators, engineers, and support personnel, all working together to advance our understanding of the universe.

829.

Lowell Observatory has been featured in various films and documentaries, highlighting its scientific contributions and historical significance.

830.

The observatory collaborates with other research institutions and observatories worldwide, fostering international partnerships and facilitating global scientific collaborations.

831.

Lowell Observatory is involved in ongoing research on the potential for asteroid impacts on Earth and the development of methods to detect and mitigate such threats.

832.

The observatory's astronomers have conducted extensive studies on the structure and evolution of galaxies, shedding light on the formation of stars, galaxies, and the large-scale structure of the universe.

833.

Lowell Observatory has a visitor center that houses interactive exhibits, multimedia presentations, and a gift shop where visitors can purchase astronomy-related merchandise.

834.

The observatory's astronomers are actively involved in the search for gravitational waves, studying their sources and developing new techniques to detect these elusive phenomena.

835.

Lowell Observatory is a member of the Association of Universities for Research in Astronomy (AURA) and collaborates with other renowned observatories and research institutions worldwide.

836.

The observatory's historic campus has been designated as a National Historic Landmark, recognizing its historical and cultural significance in the field of astronomy.

837.

Lowell Observatory played a critical role in mapping the Moon's surface during the Apollo missions, assisting NASA in selecting safe landing sites for the astronauts.

838.

The observatory's astronomers have made significant contributions to our understanding of the formation and evolution of planetary systems, including studying the debris disks around young stars.

839.

Lowell Observatory operates a state-of-the-art solar observatory, allowing scientists to study the Sun's activity and phenomena such as solar flares and sunspots.

840.

The observatory's astronomers actively participate in public outreach events, giving presentations, leading stargazing sessions, and sharing their knowledge and passion for astronomy with the community.

841.

Lowell Observatory has been at the forefront of studying Pluto and its moons. Its researchers have conducted detailed observations and measurements of the dwarf planet's surface and atmosphere.

842.

The observatory's astronomers have made significant contributions to the study of stellar populations, investigating the distribution and properties of stars in different regions of our galaxy and beyond.

843.

Lowell Observatory has a long tradition of supporting early-career astronomers through its research fellowship programs, providing them with opportunities to conduct independent research.

844.

The observatory's staff actively participates in citizen science initiatives, encouraging the public to contribute to scientific research by collecting data and reporting observations.

845.

Lowell Observatory offers a variety of educational resources for teachers, including curriculum materials, workshops, and professional development opportunities, to enhance science education in classrooms.

846.

The observatory collaborates with local schools and universities, providing students with hands-on learning experiences, internships, and access to cutting-edge astronomical research.

847.

Lowell Observatory is committed to preserving its historical artifacts and maintaining its heritage sites, ensuring that future generations can appreciate the observatory's rich history.

848.

The observatory's astronomers have conducted extensive studies on the dynamics and evolution of galaxies, examining their interactions, mergers, and the growth of supermassive black holes at their centers.

849.

Lowell Observatory has a public observatory where visitors can observe celestial objects through telescopes and engage with astronomers to learn more about the universe.

850.

The observatory's astronomers actively contribute to public outreach through social media, blogs, and podcasts, sharing their research findings, astronomical discoveries, and inspiring stories of exploration with a wider audience.

851.

The C. Hart Merriam Base Camp Site is located in Yosemite National Park, California.

852.

It was the base camp for C. Hart Merriam, an American biologist and naturalist, during his field studies in the late 19th century.

853.

Merriam conducted extensive research on the flora, fauna, and ecosystems of the Sierra Nevada region.

854.

The base camp site served as a hub for scientific exploration and data collection, contributing to our understanding of the natural history of the area.

855.

Merriam's research at the base camp site laid the foundation for the field of biogeography, studying the distribution of species in relation to environmental factors.

856.

The campsite is located in a pristine natural environment, surrounded by towering granite cliffs, lush forests, and pristine alpine meadows.

857.

The site offers breathtaking views of Yosemite Valley and the surrounding mountain ranges.

858.

It is an important historical landmark, showcasing the pioneering work of C. Hart Merriam and his contributions to scientific knowledge.

859.

The campsite is accessible via hiking trails, allowing visitors to explore the same landscapes that Merriam once studied.

860.

The area is home to a diverse range of plant and animal species, including rare and endemic species found only in the Sierra Nevada region.

861.

The base camp site provides opportunities for birdwatching, with numerous bird species inhabiting the area, including owls, woodpeckers, and songbirds.

862.

The site offers a peaceful and serene atmosphere, ideal for nature enthusiasts and those seeking solitude in the wilderness.

863.

Visitors can explore the nearby streams and rivers, which are home to various fish species, such as rainbow trout and brown trout.

864.

The campsite is an excellent spot for stargazing, with minimal light pollution and clear night skies.

865.

The area is rich in cultural history, with evidence of past Native American settlements and their use of the land.

866.

The campsite is surrounded by hiking trails, providing opportunities for outdoor recreation and exploration of the surrounding natural beauty.

867.

Wildlife sightings are common in the area, including deer, coyotes, squirrels, and various small mammals.

868.

The campsite offers a rustic camping experience, with limited facilities and a focus on immersing oneself in nature.

869.

The site is a popular destination for nature photographers, with abundant photo opportunities of the stunning landscapes and wildlife.

870.

It is important to practice Leave No Trace principles when visiting the campsite to preserve the natural environment and ensure its protection for future generations.

871.

The base camp site serves as a reminder of the early days of scientific exploration and the dedication of researchers like C. Hart Merriam.

872.

The area is known for its wildflower displays in the spring and summer months, with colorful blooms dotting the meadows and hillsides.

873.

The campsite is located near important geological features, including granite domes, glacially carved valleys, and ancient sequoia groves.

874.

Visitors can learn about the research methods and techniques used by C. Hart Merriam and gain insight into the field of ecology and natural history.

875.

The campsite offers opportunities for solitude and reflection, allowing visitors to disconnect from the hustle and bustle of everyday life.

876.

The area is a haven for outdoor enthusiasts, with nearby activities including hiking, fishing, camping, and wildlife watching.

877.

The base camp site is a designated historical site, protected and preserved for its scientific and cultural significance.

878.

The campsite is accessible by a short hike, offering a sense of adventure and exploration.

879.

Visitors can discover and appreciate the unique plant communities that thrive in the Sierra Nevada, including giant sequoias, Jeffrey pines, and alpine wildflowers.

880.

The site is a living laboratory for studying the effects of climate change on mountain ecosystems and species distribution patterns.

881.

The campsite provides an opportunity to learn about the interconnectedness of nature and the delicate balance of ecosystems.

882.

The area is part of the ancestral lands of Indigenous peoples, who have a deep cultural connection to the land and its resources.

883.

The campsite is located at an elevation that provides cooler temperatures during the summer months, offering a respite from the heat.

884.

The site is a great starting point for exploring other parts of
Yosemite National Park, including iconic landmarks like Half Dome
and Yosemite Falls.

885.

The campsite offers a peaceful retreat away from the crowds,
providing a more intimate experience of Yosemite's natural beauty.

886.

The area is rich in geological features, including exposed rock
formations, glacial erratics, and evidence of past volcanic activity.

887.

The campsite is an excellent location for nature journaling and
sketching, allowing visitors to capture the essence of the landscape
on paper.

888.

The site is part of ongoing scientific research, with ecologists and
biologists studying the ecosystem dynamics and changes over time.

889.

The campsite is open to visitors year-round, with each season
offering a unique experience, from wildflowers in spring to snow-
covered landscapes in winter.

890.

The area is home to various bird species of prey, including hawks,
eagles, and falcons, soaring through the skies above.

891.

The campsite provides opportunities for educational programs and
workshops, allowing visitors to deepen their understanding of the
natural world.

892.

The site has designated picnic areas, perfect for enjoying a meal amidst the scenic surroundings.

893.

Visitors may encounter evidence of past human activities in the area, such as old mining sites or remnants of historic structures.

894.

The campsite is located within the habitat range of black bears, and visitors should take precautions to properly store food and maintain a safe distance.

895.

The site is part of a network of protected areas, contributing to the conservation of biodiversity and the preservation of natural landscapes.

896.

The campsite is a place of inspiration, evoking a sense of wonder and awe at the beauty and complexity of the natural world.

897.

The area is home to a diverse array of fungi species, with mushroom enthusiasts enjoying forays to discover rare and fascinating specimens.

898.

The campsite offers opportunities for wildlife tracking, with animal footprints and signs providing insights into the presence and behavior of different species.

899.

The site has historical markers and interpretive signs, providing information about the natural and cultural history of the area.

900.

The campsite allows visitors to reconnect with nature, fostering a sense of stewardship and appreciation for the Earth's natural resources.

901.

John Penn was born on May 17, 1741, in Caroline County, Virginia.

902.

He was an American lawyer and politician who played a significant role in the American Revolutionary War and the formation of the United States.

903.

Penn studied law and was admitted to the bar in Virginia before moving to North Carolina.

904.

He served as a delegate to the Continental Congress from North Carolina from 1775 to 1780.

905.

Penn was one of the signers of the United States Declaration of Independence, representing North Carolina.

906.

He was the first delegate from North Carolina to sign the Declaration of Independence, signing his name on August 2, 1776.

907.

Penn was known for his eloquent speaking skills and his passionate advocacy for independence.

908.

During his time in the Continental Congress, he actively participated in debates and discussions on key issues.

909.

In addition to his role in the Continental Congress, Penn also served in the North Carolina General Assembly and held various judicial positions.

910.

He was known for his strong commitment to the principles of liberty and the rights of individuals.

911.

Penn was a staunch supporter of the Revolutionary cause and played a vital role in rallying support for independence in North Carolina.

912.

He was involved in drafting the North Carolina Constitution, which was adopted in 1776, and helped establish the new state government.

913.

After the war, Penn continued his public service and was appointed as a judge on the North Carolina Superior Court.

914.

He was instrumental in the ratification of the United States Constitution by North Carolina in 1789.

915.

Penn served as a Federalist member of the United States House of Representatives from 1789 to 1795.

916.

He supported the creation of a strong federal government and was involved in the development of early legislation.

917.

Penn was an advocate for the protection of individual rights and was known for his commitment to constitutional principles.

918.

He retired from politics in 1795 and returned to his law practice in North Carolina.

919.

Throughout his career, Penn was respected for his integrity, legal expertise, and dedication to public service.

920.

He was known for his modesty and humility, often shying away from personal recognition and preferring to focus on the greater good.

921.

Penn was deeply committed to his home state of North Carolina and played an active role in its early development.

922.

He was involved in land surveys and land acquisition, contributing to the growth and expansion of the state.

923.

Penn was a firm believer in education and supported the establishment of schools and universities in North Carolina.

924.

He was a strong proponent of religious freedom and played a role in securing religious liberty protections in the state.

925.

Penn's contributions to the American Revolution and the formation of the United States were significant but often overshadowed by his more prominent peers.

926.

He lived a relatively quiet life outside of politics, focusing on his family and legal career.

927.

Penn married Susannah Lyne in 1763, and they had three children together.

928.

He was a devoted family man and cherished his time with his wife and children.

929.

Penn's health declined in his later years, and he passed away on September 14, 1788, at the age of 47.

930.

He was buried in the churchyard of the Christ Episcopal Church in Guilford County, North Carolina.

931.

Penn's legacy as a signer of the Declaration of Independence and his contributions to the early years of the United States are commemorated and honored.

932.

His name is inscribed on the Founding Fathers of the United States memorial in Washington, D.C.

933.

Penn's home in North Carolina, known as "The Sign of the Revolution," is preserved as a historic site and museum.

934.

He is remembered as a principled and dedicated patriot who played a vital role in shaping the American nation.

935.

Penn's commitment to liberty and justice continues to inspire and influence future generations of Americans.

936.

His role as a founding father of the United States reflects his commitment to the principles of democracy and freedom.

937.

Penn's contributions to the development of the United States Constitution helped establish a strong and enduring government.

938.

His support for a centralized government balanced with individual rights remains an important aspect of American political thought.

939.

Penn's advocacy for religious freedom laid the foundation for the First Amendment's protections of religious liberty.

940.

His dedication to public service serves as an example for future leaders, emphasizing the importance of integrity and commitment to the greater good.

941.

Penn's work in the Continental Congress contributed to the unity and strength of the American colonies during the Revolutionary War.

942.

His participation in the drafting of the North Carolina Constitution ensured the establishment of a democratic state government.

943.

Penn's legal expertise and commitment to justice made him a respected figure within the legal community.

944.

He believed in the power of education to uplift individuals and society and supported efforts to expand educational opportunities.

945.

Penn's quiet and humble demeanor belied his significant contributions to the American Revolution and the early years of the nation.

946.

His commitment to individual rights and freedoms helped shape the American concept of liberty.

947.

Penn's dedication to the principles of the Enlightenment and his belief in the potential of a democratic society influenced his political views.

948.

His willingness to put the interests of the nation above personal gain or recognition reflects his strong sense of duty and patriotism.

949.

Penn's role in the ratification of the United States Constitution ensured the continued success and stability of the young nation.

950.

His life and career demonstrate the importance of individuals taking an active role in shaping the destiny of their country.

951.

Philip Syng Physick was born on July 7, 1768, in Philadelphia, Pennsylvania.

952.

He is often referred to as the "Father of American Surgery" due to his significant contributions to the field.

953.

Physick came from a family of silversmiths, but he decided to pursue a medical career instead.

954.

He studied medicine at the University of Pennsylvania and graduated in 1790.

955.

Physick continued his medical education in Europe, studying under renowned physicians and surgeons.

956.

He returned to Philadelphia in 1794 and established a successful medical practice.

957.

Physick was known for his expertise in surgery, particularly in the fields of abdominal surgery and orthopedics.

958.

He developed innovative surgical techniques and instruments, revolutionizing the practice of surgery in the United States.

959.

Physick performed the first successful removal of a gallbladder in the United States in 1802.

960.

He introduced the use of rubber gloves during surgery to prevent infection, a practice that is still followed today.

961.

Physick was a pioneer in the field of medical education and training. He established the first medical school in the United States and served as its first professor of surgery.

962.

He emphasized the importance of practical training and hands-on experience for medical students.

963.

Physick was a mentor to many aspiring physicians and influenced the development of the medical profession in the United States.

964.

He was also known for his compassionate and patient-centered approach to medicine.

965.

Physick treated patients from all walks of life, including the poor and underserved.

966.

He was involved in philanthropic efforts to improve healthcare access and quality in Philadelphia.

967.

Physick was a member of various medical societies and served in leadership roles, contributing to the advancement of medical knowledge and practice.

968.

He published several papers and books on medical topics, sharing his expertise and insights with the medical community.

969.

Physick's reputation as a skilled and innovative surgeon attracted patients from across the United States and even internationally.

970.

He was highly respected by his peers and received numerous accolades for his contributions to medicine.

971.

Physick's legacy as a surgeon and educator is commemorated in various ways, including the naming of medical buildings and awards in his honor.

972.

He played a significant role in shaping the development of surgery as a specialized field within medicine.

973.

Physick was known for his meticulous attention to detail and his precision in surgical procedures.

974.

He was also a proponent of using anesthesia during surgery, advocating for the use of ether and chloroform.

975.

Physick's contributions extended beyond surgery. He made important advancements in the field of obstetrics and gynecology as well.

976.

He developed new techniques for managing difficult childbirths and treating gynecological conditions.

977.

Physick was a proponent of medical ethics and emphasized the importance of maintaining professional standards and integrity.

978.

He believed in the continuous pursuit of knowledge and encouraged lifelong learning among physicians.

979.

Physick's dedication to patient care and safety made him a trusted and sought-after physician.

980.

He was known for his calm and steady demeanor in the operating room, which helped put patients at ease.

981.

Physick's influence on American medicine extended beyond his lifetime, as many of his students went on to become leaders in the field.

982.

He contributed to the development of medical infrastructure in Philadelphia, including the establishment of hospitals and medical societies.

983.

Physick was a lifelong learner and remained curious about new scientific and medical discoveries throughout his career.

984.

He was an advocate for public health initiatives and supported efforts to improve sanitation and hygiene practices.

985.

Physick was a dedicated family man and had a happy marriage with his wife, Henrietta.

986.

He had several children and instilled in them a love for learning and medicine.

987.

Physick enjoyed a reputation as a kind and generous person, always willing to help those in need.

988.

He was actively involved in the community and participated in charitable endeavors.

989.

Physick's surgical skills and innovations gained international recognition, and he was invited to give lectures and demonstrations in Europe.

990.

He was a member of various prestigious medical societies, both in the United States and abroad.

991.

Physick's contributions to medical education helped establish Philadelphia as a leading center for medical training in the United States.

992.

He was a strong advocate for the advancement of medical research and supported the establishment of scientific journals.

993.

Physick's expertise extended to the field of dentistry, and he made significant contributions to dental surgery and oral health.

994.

He developed new techniques for dental extractions and treatment of oral diseases.

995.

Physick's commitment to patient comfort led him to improve methods of pain management during surgery.

996.

He introduced the use of ligatures to control bleeding during surgical procedures, reducing the risk of complications.

997.

Physick's work in the field of surgery helped elevate the status of American medicine on the global stage.

998.

He was known for his dedication to teaching and mentoring future generations of physicians, leaving a lasting impact on medical education.

999.

Physick's achievements were recognized with numerous awards and honors during his lifetime.

1000.

His legacy as a pioneer in American surgery continues to inspire and influence surgeons and medical professionals today.

www.ingramcontent.com/pod-product-compliance
Lightning Source LLC
Chambersburg PA
CBHW061649250726
48659CB00004B/1435